T0301940

An Analysis of

William Cronon's

Nature's Metropolis

Chicago And The Great West

Cheryl Hudson

Published by Macat International Ltd
24:13 Coda Centre, 189 Munster Road, London SW6 6AW.

Distributed exclusively by Routledge
2 Park Square, Milton Park, Abingdon, Oxon OX14 4RN
711 Third Avenue, New York, NY 10017, USA

Routledge is an imprint of the Taylor & Francis Group, an informa business

www.macat.com
info@macat.com

Cataloguing in Publication Data
A catalogue record for this book is available from the British Library.
Library of Congress Cataloguing-in-Publication Data is available upon request.
Cover illustration: Etienne Gilfillan

ISBN 978-1-912302-46-8 (hardback)
ISBN 978-1-912128-92-1 (paperback)
ISBN 978-1-912281-34-3 (e-book)

Notice
The information in this book is designed to orientate readers of the work under analysis,
to elucidate and contextualise its key ideas and themes, and to aid in the development
of critical thinking skills. It is not meant to be used, nor should it be used, as a
substitute for original thinking or in place of original writing or research. References and
notes are provided for informational purposes and their presence does not constitute
endorsement of the information or opinions therein. This book is presented solely for
educational purposes. It is sold on the understanding that the publisher is not engaged
to provide any scholarly advice. The publisher has made every effort to ensure that
this book is accurate and up-to-date, but makes no warranties or representations with
regard to the completeness or reliability of the information it contains. The information
and the opinions provided herein are not guaranteed or warranted to produce particular
results and may not be suitable for students of every ability. The publisher shall not be
liable for any loss, damage or disruption arising from any errors or omissions, or from
the use of this book, including, but not limited to, special, incidental, consequential or
other damages caused, or alleged to have been caused, directly or indirectly, by the
information contained within.

CONTENTS

THE MACAT LIBRARY

The Macat Library is a series of unique academic explorations of seminal works in the humanities and social sciences – books and papers that have had a significant and widely recognised impact on their disciplines. It has been created to serve as much more than just a summary of what lies between the covers of a great book. It illuminates and explores the influences on, ideas of, and impact of that book. Our goal is to offer a learning resource that encourages critical thinking and fosters a better, deeper understanding of important ideas.

Each publication is divided into three Sections: Influences, Ideas, and Impact. Each Section has four Modules. These explore every important facet of the work, and the responses to it.

This Section-Module structure makes a Macat Library book easy to use, but it has another important feature. Because each Macat book is written to the same format, it is possible (and encouraged!) to cross-reference multiple Macat books along the same lines of inquiry or research. This allows the reader to open up interesting interdisciplinary pathways.

To further aid your reading, lists of glossary terms and people mentioned are included at the end of this book (these are indicated by an asterisk [*] throughout) – as well as a list of works cited.

Macat has worked with the University of Cambridge to identify the elements of critical thinking and understand the ways in which six different skills combine to enable effective thinking.
Three allow us to fully understand a problem; three more give us the tools to solve it. Together, these six skills make up the **PACIER** model of critical thinking. They are:

ANALYSIS – understanding how an argument is built
EVALUATION – exploring the strengths and weaknesses of an argument
INTERPRETATION – understanding issues of meaning

CREATIVE THINKING – coming up with new ideas and fresh connections
PROBLEM-SOLVING – producing strong solutions
REASONING – creating strong arguments

To find out more, visit **WWW.MACAT.COM.**

CRITICAL THINKING AND *NATURE'S METROPOLIS*

Primary critical thinking skill: PROBLEM-SOLVING
Secondary critical thinking skill: INTERPRETATION

What caused the rise of Chicago, and how did the city's expansion fuel the westward movement of the American frontier – and influence the type of society that evolved as a result?

Nature's Metropolis emerged as a result of William Cronon asking and answering those questions, and the work can usefully be seen as an extended example of the critical thinking skill of problem-solving in action. Cronon navigates a path between the followers of Frederick Jackson Turner, author of the thesis that American character was shaped by the experience of the frontier, and revisionists who sought to suggest that the rugged individualism Turner depicted as a creation of life in the West was little but a fiction. For Cronon, the most productive question to ask was not whether or not men forged in the liberty-loving furnace of the Wild West had the sort of impact on America that Turner posited, but the quite different one of how capitalism and political economy had combined to drive the westward expansion of the US. For Cronon, individualism was scarcely even possible in a capitalist machine in which humans were little more than cogs, and the needs and demands of capital, not capitalists, prevailed.

Nature's Metropolis, then, is a work in which the rise of Chicago is explained by generating alternative possibilities, and one that uses a rigorous study of the evidence to decide between competing solutions to the problem. It is also a fine work of interpretation, for a large part of Cronon's argument revolves around his attempt to define exactly what is rural, and what urban, and how the two interact to create a novel economic force.

ABOUT THE AUTHOR OF THE ORIGINAL WORK

Born in 1954, **William Cronon** is the Frederick Jackson Turner and Vilas Research Professor of History, Geography, and Environmental Studies at the University of Wisconsin–Madison – the same university that he attended as an undergraduate. In 2012, he served as president of the American Historical Association and is widely regarded as the founder of modern environmental history. One of his most famous works, *Nature's Metropolis: Chicago and the Great West*, won the prestigious 1992 Bancroft Prize.am's ideas in his 1995 State of the Union address.

ABOUT THE AUTHORS OF THE ANALYSIS

Dr Cheryl Hudson holds a PhD in history from Vanderbilt University, where her work examined the political culture of Chicago, 1890-1930. Currently a University Teacher in American history at the University of Liverpool, Hudson has taught at universities in the UK and the USA, including Oxford, Sheffield, Coventry, Vanderbilt, Sussex and Kent, and is a former director of the academic programme at the Rothermere American Institute, University of Oxford.

ABOUT MACAT

GREAT WORKS FOR CRITICAL THINKING

Macat is focused on making the ideas of the world's great thinkers accessible and comprehensible to everybody, everywhere, in ways that promote the development of enhanced critical thinking skills.

It works with leading academics from the world's top universities to produce new analyses that focus on the ideas and the impact of the most influential works ever written across a wide variety of academic disciplines. Each of the works that sit at the heart of its growing library is an enduring example of great thinking. But by setting them in context – and looking at the influences that shaped their authors, as well as the responses they provoked – Macat encourages readers to look at these classics and game-changers with fresh eyes. Readers learn to think, engage and challenge their ideas, rather than simply accepting them.

"Macat offers an amazing first-of-its-kind tool for interdisciplinary learning and research. Its focus on works that transformed their disciplines and its rigorous approach, drawing on the world's leading experts and educational institutions, opens up a world-class education to anyone."

Andreas Schleicher
Director for Education and Skills, Organisation for Economic Co-operation and Development

'Macat is taking on some of the major challenges in university education … They have drawn together a strong team of active academics who are producing teaching materials that are novel in the breadth of their approach.'

Prof Lord Broers,
former Vice-Chancellor of the University of Cambridge

'The Macat vision is exceptionally exciting. It focuses upon new modes of learning which analyse and explain seminal texts which have profoundly influenced world thinking and so social and economic development. It promotes the kind of critical thinking which is essential for any society and economy. This is the learning of the future.'

Rt Hon Charles Clarke, former UK Secretary of State for Education

'The Macat analyses provide immediate access to the critical conversation surrounding the books that have shaped their respective discipline, which will make them an invaluable resource to all of those, students and teachers, working in the field.'

Professor William Tronzo, University of California at San Diego

WAYS IN TO THE TEXT

KEY POINTS

- William Cronon is an American environmental historian who specializes in the history of human interactions with nature in the western region of the United States.

- Published in 1991, his book *Nature's Metropolis* argues that the city of Chicago, and settlement of the frontier lands around it, developed over time through mutual interactions.

- *Nature's Metropolis* helped launch environmental history* (the study of the historical impact of human action on nature) as an independent field of study and made the field key to both Western and US history. The book is now regarded as a classic work.

Who Is William Cronon?

William Cronon, the author of *Nature's Metropolis: Chicago and the Great West* (1991), was born in 1954 in the city of New Haven, Connecticut. He took his first degree in history at the University of Wisconsin–Madison and completed his graduate work at Yale University in the US and Oxford University in England. He is currently the Frederick Jackson Turner and Vilas Research Professor of History, Geography, and Environmental Studies at the University of Wisconsin–Madison. His father, the historian Dr. E. David Cronon,* exerted a strong influence on his career choices. William Cronon has won prestigious prizes for his teaching and publications. His academic peers elected him president of the American Historical Association in 2012.

As a boy, he spent many happy summers visiting his grandparents in rural Wisconsin—but the nearby city of Chicago haunted his imagination as a dark, dirty, and wholly unpleasant place. The Cronon family moved to Madison, Wisconsin, the state capital, when William was eight. As he grew up, he began to understand the economic and social connections between the city and countryside. His book responds to his childhood confusion about the separateness of city and country, and seeks to revise his immature judgments about each. He assumes others, including his readers, share his earlier confusion.

A finalist for the prestigious Pulitzer Prize in History and winner of the 1992 Bancroft Prize, an important literary prize awarded for books about American history, *Nature's Metropolis: Chicago and the Great West* is Cronon's second major work. It was published in 1991 while Cronon was a professor at Yale. His first book, *Changes in the Land: Indians, Colonists, and the Ecology of New England*, won the Francis Parkman Prize (another highly regarded literary prize awarded to works dealing with history). Both books have influenced the developing field of environmental history.

What Does Nature's Metropolis Say?

In *Nature's Metropolis*, William Cronon asks two crucial questions, among many:

- What role did the city of Chicago play in the dynamic development of the American West?
- How do the growth of Chicago and the development of its rural hinterland relate to one another?

Though urban history appears unrelated to the history of the natural environment, Cronon unites the two by examining Chicago's place in the development of the continental United States. By blurring the boundaries between city and countryside, Cronon illuminates their many connections; his broad research questions are driven by a desire to overturn binary and arbitrary oppositions such as that of city/country, urban/rural, and human/natural. Understanding how each side of these pairings depend upon its opposite helps historians to better grasp the many meanings within history.

Cronon acknowledges the towering influence of the historian Frederick Jackson Turner's* studies of the western United States. Western historians had largely abandoned Turner's classic 1893 work *The Significance of the Frontier in American History*, but Cronon's book mines Turner's work for its rhetorical and narrative power. While he questions its evolutionary theory of development, Cronon retains Turner's understanding that this period of history was one of transformation.

Cronon uses geographical concepts and theories to locate Chicago within a broader regional development. In particular, he shows how Chicago worked as the region's central marketplace, functioning as an engine for economic and cultural development. Cronon aims to demystify the role of capitalist* economics and expose market connections that link the city and countryside. The urban–rural relationship lies at the heart of Cronon's connection between the rise of Chicago and the development of the frontier. For Cronon, the city fueled regional transformation; it did not simply benefit from it as Turner had suggested.

Historians continue to praise Cronon's book for bringing environmental questions into Western history, thereby reinvigorating the field in many ways. Moreover, Cronon's scholarly arguments have influenced public discussions about the environment, as his work tempers the environmentalist's portrayal of human activity as destructive to the natural world.

Instead, Cronon demonstrates the human creativity nature has fostered and facilitated: by transforming nature, Americans transformed themselves. He ultimately argues that the welfare of humanity and the natural world depend on each other, so we need to look after both.

In the wake of the book's accolades and prizes, interest in environmental history and issues remain high.

Why Does Nature's Metropolis Matter?

Nature's Metropolis secured its place as a defining text in the new field of environmental history soon after its publication. Historians of the western United States and American historians generally hold it in high regard.

Nature's Metropolis is more than a simple regional or urban history. Cronon sought first to insert nature back into the history of America. He does so by framing an important debate about the character of the frontier. His analysis carries great weight because it refreshes the discussion of Turner's nineteenth-century "frontier thesis"*—the argument that American settlers' engagement with the wilderness deeply marked the country's national character, particularly with regard to notions of democracy, equality, and individualism.

While historians had largely abandoned Turner's approach, it still retained influence in popular versions of American history. Cronon attempts to bridge the divide between academic and popular history on this subject.

Where Turner saw the process of frontier development *end* with the construction of the city, Cronon's analysis *begins* with the city. He argues that people living on Turner's frontier would not, perhaps, have recognized Turner's version of events. The "urban boosters,"* for example—businessmen and city officials who sought to "boost" their city's status by public pronouncements—did not see Chicago as the result of regional development, progress, and profit, but as the engine of this change.

Finding a middle ground between Turner and the urban boosters,

Cronon charts the process of Chicago spreading outward as the environment was altered through the transformative workings of capitalism.

Cronon interpreted the link between Chicago's growth and the city's relationship with its hinterland (that is, its rural and less accessible surroundings) as a model for other historical analyses. His method and approach challenge what he sees as an arbitrary divide: the focus on Chicago as a distinct city and the territory known as "the West" as a discrete region.

His book probes the relationship between the city and the region rather than focusing on one or the other—or on both areas in isolation. This original approach alters the way historians study and understand cities and their natural surroundings.

Nature's Metropolis is a broad, ambitious project that aims to redefine the relationship between humanity and nature. In doing this, Cronon's project is culturally specific, written for a society that has lost faith in industrialization* (that is, the process of mechanizing labor, and a movement away from agriculture), market capitalism (those aspects of the dominant economic system of the West in which goods are distributed and money is exchanged for the sake of profit), and human progress.

Thus, few people before the late twentieth century could have identified with Cronon's environmentalist argument. But in the early twenty-first century, *Nature's Metropolis* retains its relevance. It challenges ingrained ideas about the relationship between humanity and nature—reminding us of the close (even if obscured) connections between urban and rural life.

Inside and outside of academia, Cronon has worked as both scholar and citizen to reinforce the arguments in his book. In particular, he claims that it is neither possible nor desirable to preserve a pristine, untouched natural environment. His book has also made an impact on a broader cultural level, deepening the ways in which poststructural theory* has permeated outlook and opinion.

Poststructural theory holds that binary oppositions such as rural/urban, being artificial constructs, are not useful to the analysis of social or linguistic systems—which is to say that Cronon works to get beyond the "either/or" dynamic that has dominated thinking about history and society.

His book has informed public policy and shaped the goals of environmental reform, while offering a critique of the workings of capitalism. In doing this, Cronon reinforces recent arguments against capitalism as an agent of change, a position that resonates with the contemporary Occupy movement* and its call for social justice.

Nature's Metropolis provides intellectual justification and moral support to environmental reformers and anti-capitalist activists.

SECTION 1
INFLUENCES

MODULE 1
THE AUTHOR AND THE HISTORICAL CONTEXT

KEY POINTS

- *Nature's Metropolis* helped launch the field of environmental history,* which considers the ways human beings have historically impacted nature and is now among the most dominant areas of historical study.

- Though William Cronon's father significantly influenced his work as a historian, the thinking he expresses in *Nature's Metropolis* was developed as a graduate student at Yale.

- The rise in popularity of environmental politics shaped Cronon's approach to history.

Why Read This Text?

William Cronon's *Nature's Metropolis: Chicago and the Great West* is an innovative piece of scholarship that unites two important fields: the history of the American West and US urban history. It also helped develop the emerging field of environmental history. The book's title intentionally implies that Chicago sprang from the bounty of nature found on the American frontier, and was not the product of artificial, human endeavor. Thus it suggests that the concepts of urban and rural depend on one another—and should not be separate areas of study.

Cronon highlights how Chicago's explosive growth in the second half of the nineteenth century and the settlement of the western United States ("the West") were intricately linked, and provides an environmental history of Chicago's rise to prominence as a great American city.

The work matters because historical discussions about the American frontier had previously overlooked the interdependence of

> **❝** Like many who came to adult consciousness during the environmentalist awakening of the late sixties, I wished to live close to nature ... Chicago represented all that was most unnatural about human life. **❞**
>
> William Cronon, *Nature's Metropolis: Chicago and the Great West*

countryside and city (or nature and civilization). While *Nature's Metropolis* belongs in the field of environmental history it helped to create, the book also pays a lot of attention to questions of economics, particularly the ways in which desire for profit drove transformations of the environment.

Cronon is most interested in the relationships constructed by the capitalist market* (that is, the mechanism by which goods and money are exchanged for the sake of profit for merchants and manufacturers); the relationships he examined were those between people and nature and between urban and rural dwellers.

But while his book is important both for its emphasis on the broad structures of the economic system of capitalism* and its focus on environmental change, it is mostly renowned for its poststructuralist* approach. Following this theoretical position, it takes aim at the acceptance of strict opposites—in this case, the city and nature.

Author's Life

William Cronon was born into an academic family and followed in the footsteps of his father, the historian E. David Cronon.* Both father and son took their undergraduate degrees in history and worked for the bulk of their careers at the University of Wisconsin–Madison, with short initial periods at Yale University; William was also awarded the prestigious Rhodes scholarship for study in England, at Oxford University.

Cronon's historical scholarship is rooted in the activist, public-oriented culture associated with the University of Wisconsin, where he is currently the Frederick Jackson Turner and Vilas Research Professor of History, Geography and Environmental Studies (his father served as the history department chair). Cronon discusses family influences at some length in *Nature's Metropolis*, and even crafts the book around his biographical story. His father encouraged him to understand that everything has a history, including naturally occurring phenomena.

Two new trends in the field emerged while Cronon was a graduate student: the New Western history* (scholarship that reinvigorated frontier history through overlooked considerations of gender, race, class, and the environment) and environmental history.

At Oxford, Cronon wrote a dissertation on the history of energy consumption in Coventry (England's tenth largest city) and began to think seriously about the connections between urban history and the natural environment. He then encountered a community of like-minded historians at Yale who strove to reshape the history of the American West, notably Patricia Nelson Limerick,* Howard R. Lamar,* and John Mack Faragher.* He found his niche in environmental history, mastered the field—and then began to change it. Today, Cronon is credited with contributing to the rise of environmental history in America. Just as it shaped his thinking, he shaped the field.

Author's Background
Cronon's writing tapped into broad cultural and intellectual trends, notably environmentalism (a political movement concerned with the protection of the environment) and poststructuralism, an analytical position often applied to literature as well as history. The core ideas of *Nature's Metropolis* emerged out of the 1980s reappraisal of the American West's history. New Western historians took their cue from the New Social history,* a movement in the 1960s and 1970s that

largely used statistical analyses of large population groups to highlight broad social currents. The people in Cronon's book do not shape events; instead their lives *are shaped by* the larger economic and ecological trends he describes.

Yet *Nature's Metropolis* also shows Cronon's flair for creative synthesis as he brings poststructuralist theories into the mix.

Poststructuralists hold that since all meaning in our world is socially constructed, one must "deconstruct"* linked things to understand the relationships between them. It targets the binary oppositions we take for granted, such as city/country or humanity/ nature. He was also influenced by the "inhumanist" poet Robinson Jeffers,* an icon of the environmentalist movement and the subject of a full-length biography Cronon wrote as an undergraduate.

Just as Jeffers viewed humans as too self-centered to appreciate nature's magnificence, Cronon challenges the human-centered approach of Frederick Jackson Turner's* frontier thesis* that the American national character was formed through the taming of the wilderness. He considers Turner's thesis "Whiggish"*—that is, that it reads history as humankind's march from ignorance to enlightenment.

Cronon positions himself as an intermediary between the two men, and between humanity and nature itself. He embraces neither Jeffers's love of nature and disregard for humans nor Turner's love of humanity and disregard for nature. In the end, he could not escape the powerful ideas in Turner's frontier thesis nor the contemporary influence of the environmental movement but he worked to modify one by bringing it into contact with the other.

While New Western historians challenged traditional interpretations of the West among their colleagues, they also sought to inform public discussion. Cronon was a proponent of the public- spirited Wisconsin Idea,* which argued that academic historians had a right and a duty to connect their scholarship to social and political issues. He also challenged people to revisit the treasured principles of environmentalism—not as someone opposed to them, but as a proponent for rethinking them.

Environmental conservation and working to limit human impact on the natural world became major forces in the 1960s with the publication of the biologist Rachel Carson's* *Silent Spring*, an account of the damaging effects on animal life of pesticides. While Cronon supports these notions, he also tries to highlight human creativity as a challenge to the movement's negative views about human destructiveness.

MODULE 2
ACADEMIC CONTEXT

KEY POINTS

- US Western history is concerned with events in the western region of the United States; environmental history* is concerned with the impact of past human action on nature.

- The historian Frederick Jackson Turner's* "frontier thesis,"* which emphasized human mastery of nature, dominated historical studies of the American West for most of the twentieth century.

- Scholars of the New Social history,* who turned to scientific methods that made use of statistics in their analysis, rejected Turner. But Cronon demonstrated that rather than being irrelevant or wrong, Turner's thesis was simply one-sided.

The Work in its Context

William Cronon's *Nature's Metropolis: Chicago and the Great West* emerged from currents in American history such as New Western history,* and its emphasis on gender, class, and race.

New Western history started in the 1970s with New Social history,* which aimed to revise our understanding of accepted accounts of the past. Influenced largely by the French *Annales* school* (named for an influential journal of history), New Social historians departed from the work that earlier political historians had done on leaders and events, demarcating the slower, less dramatic movement of historical forces.

New Social historians looked for change in the deep structures of history and often adopted statistical methods to chart that change over

66 The history of the Great West is a long dialogue between the place we call a city and the place we call country. So perhaps the best vantage point from which to view that history is not with Turner, in the outermost of von Thünen's zones, but in the place where Turner himself said 'all the forces of the nation intersect.' Viewed from the banks of the Chicago River, the Great West is both an urban empire and a countryside transformed. 99

William Cronon, *Nature's Metropolis: Chicago and the Great West*

time. To them, individuals were less important than broad social trends; for example, they distrusted the earlier historical focus on political leaders or heroes as elitist. They also argued that literary sources overplayed the role of a small elite that kept such records and that more democratic, numbers-based research could better capture the historical experience of a wider demographic.

New Western historians carried over much of this thinking to studying the American frontier and the changes wrought by the American conquest of western lands. They not only concentrated on social structures but also examined the interactions between American pioneers and the land itself. Thus as they shifted human activity away from the center of their analysis, focusing instead on how humans and the natural environment interacted, they also produced a shift in their field. This led to the emergence of a new field: environmental history.

Overview of the Field

New Western historians challenged and revised the academic understanding of the frontier by emphasizing structural changes in the development of western lands. In *Nature's Metropolis*, Cronon follows commodity exchanges (focusing on the environmental implications of the economic system of capitalism)* rather than individuals of influence to understand the changing relationship between city and country.

But in crafting his views, Cronon steers clear of strict divisions. In poststructural* fashion (that is, following a theoretical approach that tends to refuse opposites), he combines New Social history with the approach it sought to revise: Frederick Jackson Turner's classic frontier thesis. As the founder of Western regional history, Turner argued that the American experience on the frontier gave rise to America's democratic traditions, habits and practices. Cronon's work engages with Turner's influential thesis at several points: it highlights the need to deepen understanding of human interactions with nature in the West, yet also notes Turner's continued hold on academic debate and the public imagination.

This line of thinking resonated with the founders of environmental history, usually cited as the historians Samuel P. Hays* (who studied the early twentieth-century conservation movement) and Roderick Nash (who charted shifting American attitudes towards American wilderness). Moreover, since environmental history was a comparatively new field, a scholar of Cronon's caliber made a strong impression, posing the questions that would define its development.

Cronon sought not to romanticize nature but to deconstruct* its meaning—especially in relationship to the "non-natural" urban environment. In other words, he begins his analysis from the poststructuralist position that meaning owes more to language than it does to any objective version of "reality."

The earliest environmental histories either studied the evolution of wilderness in the American imagination or the history of public service politics—such as those of sewage disposal or water supply—in shaping areas. Moving the field forward, Cronon asked questions about the relationship between nature and society that challenged earlier assumptions about nature's passivity and people's activity.

Academic Influences

Cronon is a leading member of the environmental history field alongside the key thinkers Richard White,* Carolyn Merchant,* and Donald Worster,* all American historians who have brought the natural world into the story of American history. Although there are differences between them, all focus on the impact of American civilization on the environment.

As well as giving the new field shape and force, Cronon has also distinguished himself as part of a group of New Western historians who reinvented the study of the American West. And indeed, there is overlap between pioneers of environmental history and New Western historians, who include White, Cronon and Worster as well as the American scholars Patricia Nelson Limerick,* Howard R. Lamar,* and John Mack Faragher.*

Yet Cronon departs from some New Western thought because he does not adopt the same scrutiny of social relationships that involve gender, race, ethnicity, and class. Instead, he focuses his attention on market mechanisms and environmental impacts. He also departs from the concerns of other environmental historians due to his strong regional focus in the West and his use of poststructural theory.

Cronon's ideas belong to both these historical schools and yet neither one entirely—a sign of his intellectual desire to break boundaries and build bridges.

MODULE 3
THE PROBLEM

KEY POINTS

- How can we explain Western history now that the historian Frederick Jackson Turner's* concept of the frontier* is no longer acceptable?

- The New Western history* recast the frontier history of the western US states by focusing on race, class, gender, and the environment, and how their meanings changed over time.

- Cronon modified both Turner's frontier myth and the new focus on the experience of social groups. He rejected binary oppositions and sought to place both the frontier and Westerners within an overarching relationship.

Core Question

When William Cronon published *Nature's Metropolis: Chicago and the Great West*, the American historical profession was in a period of flux. Uncertainty ran high about whether historical objectivity was even possible. Cronon sought to restore order to the study of the past through his book's themes and arguments, contending that while social structures were historically unstable they nevertheless had a coherent logic. His contribution to developing Western history (an established field) and environmental history* (an emerging one) helped sustain the profession as a whole. By taking on Frederick Jackson Turner's frontier thesis (which held that the American character emerged as a result of conquering the western wilderness), Cronon breathed new life into a historical narrative at the heart of debates about the American character.

Cronon revives and revises Turner's argument. Influential as it was,

25

❝ Far from being the crucible of 'Americanization' which Turner made of it, the frontier was a region where racial and ethnic minorities remained significantly isolated from other communities: Blacks, Chicanos, Chinese, and Indians all had historical experiences that meshed neither with Turner's thesis nor with the dominant culture of Turner's day, and so he failed to study them. The same was true of women. **❞**

William Cronon, "Revisiting the Vanishing Frontier: The Legacy of Frederick Jackson Turner," *The Western Historical Quarterly*

Turner's thesis had long been doubted and critiqued within the historical profession. While continuing the critique of Turner as teleological* and deterministic* (that is, Turner assumed that American history unfolded according to unavoidable and seemingly designed goals and ends), Cronon also upholds Turner's conception of the frontier as a place where interactions with nature spawned human creativity.

New Western historians had successfully challenged Turner on several fronts. First, they held that he ignored the experiences of women and racial minorities; second, they rebuked his suggestion that frontier development represented non-problematic, evolutionary social progress. Cronon, however, takes on the social concerns of Turner's challengers. He thrusts Turner back into the center of the debate by highlighting his concern with how the environment and humanity interact. However, in the process of doing so, Cronon downgrades the role of humanity and upgrades that of nature from Turner's own positions. For Turner, humans were active and nature was passive. But for Cronon, it is more difficult to distinguish between the value and power of humanity and that of nature.

The Participants

Cronon's questions are important to three fields: urban history, environmental history, and Western history.

Until *Nature's Metropolis*, urban historians largely concerned themselves with city demographics, politics, and culture, while delineating social divisions among classes and races. Cronon rejects this agenda, however, because he was more interested in the city's rural connections and less interested in people than in processes (that is, he was less concerned with individuals than in social factors such as economics).[1] Indeed, Chicagoans rarely figure in the book, except as conduits for the logic of the market relationships that fascinate Cronon.

Cronon deconstructs the urban–rural dichotomy (that is, the binary opposition of "city" and "farmland") to show that both exist only in relation to one another and depend on the other for meaning. While many might see the city as the dominant partner, Cronon demonstrates how it fully depends on its interaction with its rural hinterland—not only as a concept but also through the force of real social and economic relationships. Cronon's approach is radical and interdisciplinary (meaning it draws on the aims and methods of academic fields outside of history): it disrupts the previous contours of urban, environmental, and Western history.

Cronon's concept of Chicago's place in the Midwest region relies heavily upon the work of the nineteenth-century German economist Johann Heinrich von Thünen.* For Cronon, von Thünen's isolated state theory,* which proposes that produce is valued according to the cost of producing and transporting it from farms to the city, serves to reconcile the opposing differences between Turner's frontier thesis and that of "urban boosters"* of the late nineteenth century—businessmen and officials who looked to increase the public perception of their city as a place of worth, hoping to profit in some way. The city was neither the end of progressive evolution, as Turner surmised, nor the dynamo behind regional development, as boosters claimed. Instead, it developed—and either thrived or failed—in relation to its surrounding farmlands.

The Contemporary Debate

The intellectual uncertainty surrounding historical knowledge played out in the United States during the 1980s as the theoretically structuralist* "either-or" approaches to history gave way to poststructuralist approaches (which take apart those divisions). By using poststructuralism, Cronon could question and take apart the divides between social and natural, urban and rural, city and countryside. Yet in charting the rise of Chicago, Cronon places these categories within an overarching structure of capitalist relations—an approach generally associated with structuralist thinkers.

Given Cronon's creative use of existing ideas and theories, *Nature's Metropolis* may seem hard to pin down. That said, its interest in the analysis of human action on the environment, it most properly belongs within the field of environmental history.

As the similar title suggests, it is indebted to *Nature's Economy* by the American historian Donald Worster for its place within an intellectual school. Worster and Cronon both concentrated on the American Midwest and shaped strong connections between environmental history and the New Western history. What is more, Worster's work on the Dust Bowl* (the area of the Midwest troubled by soil erosion during the economic collapse that marked the 1930s) anticipated how Cronon would examine the historical relationship between humanity and nature. Cronon engaged with the contemporary debate about the Midwest while also reaching back to find value in Turner's frontier. His central innovation was to bring that most modern, man-made structure—the city—into juxtaposition with the natural world that surrounded it. Before Cronon, most historians would have seen them as opposing or opposite; after Cronon, it was possible to see them for the first time as complementary.

NOTES

1   William Cronon, *Nature's Metropolis: Chicago and the Great West* (New York: W.W. Norton & Co., 1992), XVII.

MODULE 4
THE AUTHOR'S CONTRIBUTION

KEY POINTS

- The city of Chicago and the Western countryside depended upon one another; their successful development was inextricably interrelated.

- *Nature's Metropolis* reinvigorated interest in the American West by making the study of its environment integral to understanding its history.

- Cronon both saved Frederick Jackson Turner's* frontier thesis* from oblivion and comprehensively buried it. Building on the work of fellow neo-Turnerians and environmental historians, he applied poststructural* theory to the analysis of Western history.

Author's Aims

With Nature's *Metropolis: Chicago and the Great West*, William Cronon seeks to integrate apparently opposing ideas and concepts into a coherent whole. From a philosophical standpoint, this meant demonstrating that the natural world and human society were ineradicably intertwined with (and dependent on) each other. Geographically, he had to show that places called "cities" and "countryside" were so strongly connected, and in so many ways, that there was no means to disconnect them. Although this is a tall order, Cronon goes further. He shows how linguistically, the terms "urban" and "rural" need one another for their existence and meaning. And within the history field itself, it meant staking a middle ground between Frederick Jackson Turner's frontier thesis and the findings and refutations of revisionist* scholars.

What emerges is an overarching, ambitious narrative in which

❝ The fusing of these analyses of the concrete and the abstract, this insistent focus on relationships, makes *Nature's Metropolis* a challenging and important book. It both participates in and transcends current intellectual trends. To the extent that this book is primarily concerned with relationships, it is a postmodern history … The book is also a salutary movement beyond postmodernism. **❞**

Richard White, "Review of Nature's Metropolis," *Environmental History Review*

human agency (the capacity of individuals to shape the future) is replaced with structure (in this analysis, that of the forces of capitalism). This serves to define Cronon's text as different from its predecessors. The book is successful at what it seeks to do, intentionally neglecting any examination of the various incentives that drove individual Americans' actions—with one notable exception. *Nature's Metropolis* suggests that the one motive for action on the American frontier was that of profit. Cronon aims to show that Americans operated as cogs in a large, impersonal political economy. The economic system of capitalism* is "the elephant in the room": an obvious but unmentioned presence, the unifier of interactions between humanity and nature, cities and countryside. The urgent needs and demands of capital, the lifeblood of capitalism, permeate the pages of the book, while the operation or even the possible exercise of human free will is absent.

Approach

Cronon participated in the broad intellectual shift away from strict dualisms. While his philosophical approach is present in many existing historical fields, Cronon used it to energize the new field of environmental history;* rather than presenting nature as passive and humans as active, Cronon highlights their mutual dependence, stressing the prior existence of nature before human involvement and highlighting the many unintended consequences of human action upon nature. In Cronon's schema (his model), neither nature nor humanity exerts any real control. Rather, the character of their interaction determines the outcome for both. At a fundamental level, humanity and nature exist as one.

Cronon also insists that it is wrong to separate the development of the city from that of the countryside. To understand the interconnections on every level, the historian must "tell the city–country story as a unified narrative."[1] By uncovering the historical relationship between the city, or "nature's metropolis," and the countryside, Cronon shows that unadulterated nature exists nowhere. Still nature itself continues to exist in the very structures and processes of urban life. Ultimately, the city was built on the fruits of its natural hinterlands; and the hinterlands thrive or fail only in relation to the city.

Contribution in Context

When William Cronon's _Nature's Metropolis_ emerged, the American historical profession was avoiding both determinism* (according to which, humans live at the mercy of external forces) and historicism* (according to which, human choices are curtailed by cultural context). Searching for an alternative ground, historians in all fields began to locate the connections and intersections between different phenomena as worthy of study in their own right. If human action was neither fully determined by external forces nor chosen freely with no reference to external forces, then perhaps, they suggested, it might operate within an interactive framework.

Some historians went even further, breaking down or "deconstructing" the barriers between previously defined dualisms. These included but were not limited to public/private, black/white and—most pertinent for Cronon—human/natural and city/countryside.

However, within the history field's debate over the nature of Western settlement, Cronon suggests that traditional concepts of the vanishing frontier still retain some validity. He concedes that the Turner's frontier myth has rightly succumbed to the creditable attacks of revisionists (those who seek to overturn orthodox historical interpretations). He is also working on a local history of Turner's hometown—Portage, Wisconsin.

Yet Cronon also seeks to defuse and moderate the criticism—while at the same time playing a major role in modifying and undermining the central thrust of Turner's thesis. He is a neo-Turnerian who transforms Turner's own emphasis on the dynamism and creativity of humanity into a focus on the transformative interactions between humans and the environment. In other words, Cronon removes the focus from human beings and places it on a process: the mutual interaction between humanity and nature. Cronon does not see a split between the two, and this creates a definitive split from Turner's thought.

He rescues Turner, only to kill him again more effectively.

NOTES

1   William Cronon, *Nature's Metropolis: Chicago and the Great West* (New York: W.W. Norton & Co., 1992), xvi.

SECTION 2
IDEAS

MODULE 5
MAIN IDEAS

KEY POINTS

* The book charts the concurrent emergence and development of the city of Chicago and the agricultural market in the city's hinterlands.

* For Cronon, Chicago did not represent an evolutionary stage within an ongoing, progressive frontier development but a "gateway city" to Western lands. City and country existed in mutual dependence and their relationship represented and reproduced American capitalism* as we know it.

* The book's key ideas are presented in three sections: the first two sections focus on the city and the countryside respectively and the final section on the overarching relationship between capital and commodity (that is, roughly, goods) that linked them.

Key Themes

Three key themes dominate William Cronon's *Nature's Metropolis: Chicago and the Great West*:

* Part one: "To Be the Central City," deals with the rise of Chicago to regional dominance.
* Part two,: "Nature to Market," traces the transformation of the rural hinterland as the market relations of the city assert themselves. It follows the impact of urban markets on crops and livestock and traces how market demand transforms their cultivation and transport to town.
* Part three: "The Geography of Capital," analyzes capital flows and explores the limits and opportunities that the logic of capital imposed on city and countryside.

❝ Since my own private passion is to understand environmental change in relation to the actions of human beings, blending as best I can the insights of ecology and economics, I have organized this book around a topic that many will initially find peculiar if not off-putting: commodity flows. ❞

William Cronon, *Nature's Metropolis: Chicago and the Great West*

By structuring the book in this way, Cronon sets up a narrative of events that starts with a focus on the city and deconstructs* its relationship with the region.

He then examines the surrounding countryside and the ways in which agricultural products became commodities in the urban market. So by looking at the relationship between the city and the country—from first one side and then the other—Cronon draws out the many ways they connect. The final section brings together urban–rural relations within the overarching structure of capitalism.*

The ordering of these themes is logical and consistent with Cronon's fundamental concern: to understand the American frontier in relation to the development of a great industrial city.

Exploring the Ideas

Cronon's argument in *Nature's Metropolis* connects the rise of Chicago and the development of the Midwest with the operation of capital within both processes. The first two sections, dealing with the city and countryside, complement each other and operate on an equal level as they examine the urban–rural relationship from each perspective. The final section works on a more general level, drawing out Cronon's theoretical positions with profit as the main driver.

In examining Chicago's rise to regional prominence, Cronon first considers the city's role on the frontier, placing Frederick Jackson

Turner's* historical explanation on one side and the contemporary commentary of urban boosters* on the other. Turner, Cronon notes, positioned the city as the end stage of frontier development and evolutionary progress: from the ax to the plough to the pulpit.[1]

Following initial settlement, civilization became increasingly complex and created cities as gleaming examples of culture and industry. Yet Cronon shows more sympathy to the claims of urban boosters, who considered their cities the engines of frontier development—and not, as Turner argued, the beneficiaries of it. Cronon suggests that the German economist Johann Heinrich von Thünen's* isolated state theory* of how agricultural goods were valued provides a more sophisticated understanding of urban–rural commercial exchange. He notes that two additional factors facilitated Chicago's domination of the region: capital investment from the Eastern US and the construction of the nation's railroad system.

To understand how urban markets transformed the surrounding countryside, Cronon follows three agricultural commodities—grain, lumber, and meat—and traces how capital restructured the ways they were raised and marketed.

The transformation is most impressive with grain: wheat and corn were transformed from physical sacks of product into pure abstractions: conceptualized, they were traded on the futures markets at the Chicago Board of Trade.*

With lumber, Cronon notes that it did not become an abstract, tradable commodity in the same way. Yet he argues that the value it brought to the market was based on its inherent value, abundance and overall use—and not on the labor used to extract it.[2]

Without forests, there could be no lumber industry and Chicago swallowed the forests to build itself up, both literally (in frame houses) and figuratively (in establishing a lumber market). Finally, meatpacking plants alienated Chicagoans from the natural process of death by making the slaughter of animals into an industrial process.

At every stage of his argument, Cronon underlines how the relationship between city and countryside, between urban markets and outlying farms, and between merchants and farmers makes up a wider framework not under the control of the individuals involved. And in the final part of the book, Cronon's overarching argument becomes more explicit. Here, he explains how the natural world (first nature)* and the alterations that humans made to it (second nature) shaped Chicago's growth. Cronon highlights how capital transformed first nature into second, while mystifying the process so that the connections between the two were obscured.

He is more concerned, however, with second nature—a "commodified" nature in which the stuff of the environment is transformed into trade goods and economic resources. He argues that second nature is often mistaken for first; this is important because for Cronon and many environmentalists, first nature carries greater authority due to its authenticity. Untouched by human hand and unsullied by the profit motive, first nature is original, pure, and true to itself.

Language and Expression

Cronon's contribution is highly original, although his formulations rest on a number of theoretical discussions historians and philosophers had already undertaken. By applying poststructuralist* concepts to the study of the frontier, Cronon brings the role of the city into a debate that was previously primarily about rural life, settlers, farmers, and the wilderness of the frontier. In this way, he reshapes the discussion entirely.

Additionally, Cronon avoids the jargon associated with poststructuralism. His lively, fluent writing engages the reader in a journey that proceeds from farm to factory and back again. His painstaking research illuminates the smallest details of agricultural production, credit extensions, and market exchange, placing them in a broader, compelling context—and as part of a larger system. As he charts the journey of sacks of wheat on barges floating down the Mississippi river to New Orleans, for example, he also locates them as symbols of the insecure, arbitrary nature of trade before Chicago rose to power.

Thereafter, as capitalist trade universalized exchange, so that all exchanges took place inside a single economic structure of growing strength and influence, grain (now transported by rail) became a flowing river of gold in Chicago elevators,* used to store grain. Sometimes his terms—such as the concepts of "first nature" and "second nature"—can obscure his meaning. Yet in his use of concrete examples, expressive language, and crisp imagery, Cronon brings his historical text to life.

NOTES

1   William Cronon, *Nature's Metropolis: Chicago and the Great West* (New York: W.W. Norton & Co., 1992), 31–32.

2   Cronon, Nature's Metropolis, 148–151.

MODULE 6
SECONDARY IDEAS

KEY POINTS

- Historically, Americans have been ambivalent in their attitudes toward the city. Railroads heralded many changes in the organization of the West. Commercialism (the culture of a capitalist* society) obscured the relationship between modern commodities and nature.

- The text's secondary ideas mainly deal with the meaning of the transformations that took place rather than the processes through which change occurred.

- The significance of Cronon's analysis of the role of railroads can be seen in the subsequent publication of fellow Western-environmentalist historian* Richard White's* book *Railroaded* (2012).

Other Ideas

William Cronon deals with several ideas in *Nature's Metropolis: Chicago and the Great West* beyond Chicago's role in developing the American frontier. He addresses the prevalence of anti-urban attitudes in the American imagination, including those he held in his younger years. He also discusses how technology impacted the history of the Midwest, particularly with the many changes that railroads brought. His focus extends from the production and distribution of commodities to their commercial distribution throughout the Midwest and nation. And Cronon's treatment of commodity fetishism*—roughly, the conception of the social relations that occur when goods are produced as economic relations between those goods themselves—is fascinating, if underdeveloped. As he points out, capital

> 66 By fulfilling the role that the railroads had assigned
> it—serving as the gateway between East and West—
> Chicago became the principal wholesale market for
> the entire midcontinent. Whether breaking up bulk
> shipments from the East or assembling bulk shipments
> from the West, it served as the entrepôt—the place
> in between—connecting eastern markets with vast
> western resource regions. 99
>
> William Cronon, *Nature's Metropolis: Chicago and the Great West*

is not a thing but a relationship.

This insight also informs his discussion of the role New York investment played in Chicago; that is, Eastern finance helped build Chicago as a gateway city to the West.

Within *Nature's Metropolis,* a number of areas merit additional focus or comment. These include a number of variously related themes:

- the book's use of Cronon's personal narrative to highlight a historical problem
- the political solutions Chicagoans developed to cope with and remedy the growth-related issues raised in the book
- a refocusing on the question of human creation and ingenuity in regards to intervention in nature.

Exploring the Ideas

Cronon attempts to untangle the reasons why Americans were so frequently ambivalent about the city in the second half of the nineteenth century. He does this first in the prologue by examining literary representations of Chicago by contemporary novelists. Then in his penultimate chapter, he notes the responses of visitors from the city's hinterlands to Chicago World's Fair in 1893 (the event, interestingly, at which Frederick Jackson Turner* first presented *The*

Significance of the Frontier in American History).

While he demonstrates the existence of widespread ambivalence—awe and horror in equal part—Cronon does not uncover the reasons for it. Instead, he relies upon a personal account of when he realized that the city was not as terrifying, fearsome, or most importantly *unnatural*, as his younger self believed. By demonstrating that Chicago was in fact part of nature (albeit second nature), Cronon traces a path to help rid Americans of their fearful anti-urban attitudes.

Many of Cronon's stories about visitors' impressions of Chicago include narratives of their arriving by rail.

It is hard to overstate how much the railroad transformed the political economy of the region. Cronon highlights, for example, how Chicago's position as a railroad hub (and not its place on the shores of Lake Michigan) helped the city outflank St. Louis in the race for regional dominance. Railroads also aided Chicago's takeover of the pork industry from "Porkopolis"—the city of Cincinnati. Cronon shows clearly how railroads brought economies of scale to Chicago and "thus became the chief device for introducing a new capitalist logic to the geography of the Great West."[1]

Chicago's rise to prominence also rested on Eastern investment rather than on its natural advantages of lake, river, and port. For New York investors in particular, Chicago was not a central city but a gateway to the Great West— where Eastern means met Western opportunity. For Midwestern farmers, however, Chicago operated as a central site for selling their own goods and purchasing the commodities of modern life. Commercial distributors such as Montgomery Ward and Sears Roebuck ultimately alienated producers from their own products by turning them into consumers and thus obscuring the connections between producer and product—thanks in large part to advertising.

Overlooked

Cronon has since written about the important role of narrative in the writing of history. He shows awareness of the ways historians might frame an understanding of the past by how they formulate and edit the story—and even where they begin and end the narrative.[2]

He encourages historians to employ narrative but in a self-conscious manner. And so there is a frank discussion to be had about why Cronon employs an autobiographical style in *Nature's Metropolis*. One reviewer commented on this with some bewilderment and not a little hostility, suggesting that Nature's Metropolis requires "more nineteenth-century Chicago and less twentieth-century Cronon."[3] A fruitful discussion would address the presentism* of Cronon's work (that is, the intrusion of present-day ideas and perspectives into historical interpretations) and ask whether this is necessary, avoidable, or desirable in historical writing as a whole.

Regardless, Cronon steps to the side as he seeks to disturb a common narrative: that human invention and creativity overcome the obstacles nature throws up against human progress.

In relation to the study of Western history, this theme (as we have seen) is often associated with Frederick Jackson Turner's frontier thesis.* As Cronon tempers this, he also uses his narrative to insert nature into the story as a historical agent alongside humanity. The political historian Robert W. Rydell* suggests that by demoting human activity, Cronon ignores the political reactions of urban and rural Midwesterners to the consequences of the market.[4] That noted, urban history provides an opportunity to draw out the full implications of Cronon's approach and methods. As they explore the mutual relationship between nature and culture within all aspects of city life, historians can potentially move past the dominant and pessimistic declensionist* narrative—that is, one of decline—regarding human impact on the environment.

Economic geographers point out that Cronon has misunderstood the distinction between value and wealth made by the economist and political theorist Karl Marx,* and this might represent a very fruitful area for future discussion and analysis. Cronon dismisses this Marxist tenet because it overlooks the value contained within first nature* (the natural world) itself. However, is Cronon correct to modify the Marxist labor theory of value, demoting the human input in favor of nature's bounty?[5] Or is he simply leaving behind old ideas of capital in order to offer new ones?

NOTES

1 *William Cronon,* Nature's Metropolis: Chicago and the Great West (New York: W.W. Norton & Co., 1992), 81; see Richard White's subsequent Railroaded: *The Transcontinentals and the Making of Modern Americ*a (W.W. Norton, 2012).

2 William Cronon, "A Place for Stories: Nature, History, and Narrative," *Journal of American History 78*, no. 4 (1992): 1347–76.

3 Howard N. Rabinowitz, "The New Western History Goes to Town, or Don't Forget That Your Urban Hamburger was Once a Rural Cow: A Review Essay," *Magazine of Western History 43*, no. 2 (1993): 73–77.

4 Robert Rydell, "Nature's Metropolis: Chicago and the Great West. By William Cronon," *Southwestern Historical Quarterly 97*.1 (1993): 169–70.

5 Brian Page and Richard Walker, "*Nature's Metropolis:* The Ghost Dance of Christaller and von Thünen," *Antipode 26*, no. 2 (1994): 152–62. Page and Walker point out that Cronon's approach disregards the historical specificity of capitalist relations (that is, that Marx's theory locates labor as the measure of value only within capitalism and not at all times).

MODULE 7
ACHIEVEMENT

KEY POINTS

- William Cronon successfully bridged and reshaped numerous fields in US history, including urban, economic, environmental,* and Western history as well as several disciplines, including geography and economics.

- Academic thinkers across all disciplines in the 1980s and 1990s were very open to poststructuralist* thought, and its propositions about language, context, and the reductive and artificial nature of binary oppositions.

- The text's broad and wide-ranging nature is both a blessing and a curse; experts from the numerous fields it touches upon are able to find fault with *Nature's Metropolis.*

Assessing the Argument

William Cronon originally published *Nature's Metropolis: Chicago and the Great West* in 1991 and the book has aged well. It is now considered a founding text of environmental history and remains highly regarded among historians of the West, as well. The popularity reflects how Cronon helped reposition these fields at the center of American history. Overall American historians have embraced *Nature's Metropolis*; those in the fields of urban and economic history, less so.

Since *Nature's Metropolis*, the field of environmental history has expanded exponentially, with William Cronon at the forefront. Few historians have taken up the issue of human–natural encounters in such a broad, innovative manner as Cronon. Yet his influence has moved some to bring the natural environment into discussions of historical issues that might otherwise have been seen as purely social or

❝ *Nature's Metropolis* is often innovative and insightful—
even when derivative—and despite its fascination with
the trappings of deconstruction and semiotics, adds
considerably to the study of urban growth and rural
transformation. **❞**

Ben Rogers and Emily Robinson, *The Benefits of Community Engagement:
A Review of the Evidence*

cultural. To be sure, the central argument of *Nature's Metropolis*—that
the difference between urban and rural landscapes collapses in the face
of capitalist market forces—has proven controversial. However, the
poststructuralist approach that underpins it has been widely praised in
numerous fields of American history. *Nature's Metropolis* was certainly
in the vanguard of a broader movement to adopt an approach that
examines the borders between things, rather than the things
themselves.

Achievement in Context

Nature's Metropolis gave added steam to the movement towards
poststructuralist models of history writing. In the field of Western
history, Cronon's work, along with the historian Richard White's*
The Middle Ground, has recast the Midwest's regional identity.[1] Part
frontier, part gateway to the American West, the region is now broadly
conceived as a place of fluid relationships as well as dynamic
interactions and cultural exchanges. As a consequence, this
understanding of the region informs most current research in
the field.

Although urban historians have not been so universally influenced
by Cronon's approach in *Nature's Metropolis*, some urban histories
adapt his claims for the important role of nature and the environment.
These have largely taken two shapes. First, some studies of particular

cities emulate Cronon's work on Chicago by employing his metropolis–hinterland thesis (originally derived from geographical theories). And second, Cronon has influenced studies that confine themselves to city environments but examine the role of natural as well as man-made environments within them.[2] The historian and political activist Mike Davis* provided a very different account of a city's relationship with the environment by placing a strong emphasis on how public policy failed to deal adequately with ecological threats.[3]

Limitations

Nature's Metropolis remains valid today but it is entirely possible readers of the future will have less use for it. The book, however, might still be applied in two ways: through use of its internal arguments; and through the methodology and approach Cronon employs.

Because the book examines a particular place and time—Chicago at the end of the nineteenth century—it is difficult to see how a similar analysis might be used in assessing the growth of other cities. To begin with, few cities have had such a massive impact upon, and codependent relationship with, their hinterlands. Also, few American urban areas have served as "gateway cities" to new, undeveloped regions. Few cities, indeed, experienced the kind of rapid growth and transformations Chicago did in relation to the surrounding countryside. So the applicability of Cronon's specific interpretation is limited by the particular subject matter.

However, Cronon sought to make his interpretation of the growth of Chicago and the city's relationship with its hinterland a model for other historical analyses. He hoped his methodology and philosophy would disrupt the previous focus on Chicago as a distinct city, and the West as a discrete region. Instead, Cronon zeroes in on the relationship between the two. This indicates that Cronon aimed to alter the way cities and their surrounding natural environments are understood by historians and contemporary readers alike. It was a broad, ambitious project and was a culturally specific project, too, in the sense that it could only be debated from within a society that has lost faith in the benefits of industrialization,* market capitalism,* and human progress in general.

Yet some historians have criticized Cronon for his misanthropy* and anthropomorphism*—that is, his apparent disdain for human influence and penchant for assigning human qualities to nature. These critics tend to come from an older generation that might remember the pain of scarcity and hunger from the days of the American economic collapse known as the Great Depression.*[4] Cronon by contrast grew up in a comfortable, middle-class home with no experience of poverty, hunger, or scarcity. Very few people before the late twentieth century could identify with Cronon's environmentalist argument.

Without question, it is of its time: post-scarcity. Will this be true of a future time, as well? That likely depends on whether human beings will shape the natural world positively—and place faith in their ability to do so without harm.

NOTES

1   Richard White, *The Middle Ground: Indians, Empires, and Republics in the Great Lakes Region*, 1650–1815 (Cambridge: Cambridge University Press, 1991).

2   An example of the approach in urban history is Richard A. Walker, The Country in the City: *The Greening of the San Francisco Bay Area* (Seattle: University of Washington Press, 2008).

3   Mike Davis, *Ecology of Fear: Los Angeles and the Imagination of Disaster* (London: Vintage Books, 1999).

4   Peter Coclanis, "Urbs in Horto," *Reviews in American History 20*, no. 1 (1992): 14–20; and Howard Rabinowitz, "The New Western History Goes to Town, Or Don't Forget That Your Urban Hamburger Was Once a Rural Cow: A Review Essay," *Montana: The Magazine of Western History 43,* no. 2 (1993): 73–77.

MODULE 8
PLACE IN THE AUTHOR'S WORK

KEY POINTS

- William Cronon's body of work investigates the history of human interactions with nature within the United States.

- *Nature's Metropolis* was a mature realization of insights apparent in Cronon's first book. He has not yet published a third major work, but his subsequent essays and articles, as well as his significant public interventions, have further developed the arguments in this book.

- *Nature's Metropolis*, following close upon the publication of *Changes in the Land*, established Cronon's reputation as a scholar of great sophistication and renown.

Positioning

William Cronon's second book, *Nature's Metropolis: Chicago and the Great West* began life as his doctoral dissertation. Sophisticated ideas and concepts abound; the book is well written and displays mastery over its subject matter. This is remarkable considering that *Nature's Metropolis* was the author's first serious academic endeavor. But it was not his first achievement of note.

Cronon's first book, *Changes in the Land: Indians, Colonists, and the Ecology of New England*, introduced him to the profession as a scholar of great originality and insight. Based on a graduate research paper, *Changes in the Land* studies property and ecology in colonial New England. It won the Francis Parkman Prize awarded by the Society of American Historians to a work of history and also proved highly influential in the developing field of environmental history.[*1] It was *Nature's Metropolis*, however, that cemented Cronon's position in

> **"** In an immensely more detailed, sophisticated, and complicated manner, *Nature's Metropolis* carries forward the central themes of Cronon's Changes in the Land: the environmental transformations brought by capitalism and the connections between environmental and social change. **"**

Richard White, Review of *Nature's Metropolis, Environmental History Review*

environmental history and the revisionist* school of New Western* history; it won him widespread recognition and a full professorship at Yale. The book is the culmination of Cronon's intellectual journey, assembling the many ideas and influences he absorbed as a student— while spotlighting his growth into a scholar of mature thinking.

Nature's Metropolis deserves, and has received, special attention from the historical profession. The reasons for this are many: its innovative, interdisciplinary approach (that is, it finds use for the methods and insights of many different academic fields); its sophisticated application of theory; its deep well of supporting evidence; and its elegant prose. The book also stands out for giving a new field of inquiry—environmental history—an elevated level of significance and importance among subfields of American history.

Integration

Following the success of *Nature's Metropolis*, Cronon won an enormous amount of intellectual and professional latitude that allowed him to pursue his intellectual interests.

First among his priorities was to promote the field of environmental history. To this end, he edited an impressive series at the University of Washington Press, containing many important studies that took a fresh look at the history of natural systems and the human influence upon them. The reputation that his two books earned also allowed Cronon to return to the University of Wisconsin–Madison, which had always been his intellectual home and better suited his citizen-as-scholar persona. In 1993, he accepted the university's Frederick Jackson Turner professorship and, a decade later, received its highest academic honor: the Vilas research professorship.

Cronon believes that scholarship and active engagement in civic affairs go hand in hand: He engages in both. In his public role, Cronon angered environmental activists and thinkers when he published an article attacking what he saw as the precious, protected, and overly romantic conceptions of "wilderness" held by many in the movement. In the essay, Cronon suggested that modern concepts of "wilderness"—imagining it as an untouched rural idyll set apart from civilization—were simply inaccurate. Instead, he argued that such views actually impeded the effective management of natural resources and prevented their preservation for future generations.

He charged environmentalists with erecting a crude, unsatisfying conflict between "human" and "nonhuman" that worked to the detriment of both people and nature.[2] Although he sparked a furious debate, he kept a firm hold of the middle ground; he worked to modify and soften the positions of conservationists on one side, and resource developers on the other. In fact, Cronon consistently seeks the middle ground in both his scholarship and public engagement.

Significance

Cronon's uppermost priority was to insert nature back into the history of the American past and he does so within the central debate about the character of the frontier. By tackling and refreshing the discussion surrounding Frederick Jackson Turner's* frontier thesis,* Cronon's analysis takes on a greater significance. Yet it does more than simply advance the work of a prominent nineteenth-century historian. The book's innovative approach to environmental history creates a fresh framework for the field of Western history, in large part due to Cronon's use of a fashionable poststructuralist* methodology. This brought Cronon and his work much professional acclaim.

Since *Nature's Metropolis*, Cronon has focused on editing, teaching, and administration as well as engaging in public citizen-scholar activities to advance progressive politics. Sometimes that has caused friction; after starting an online blog in 2011, he immediately became embroiled in a political-academic controversy.[3] His scholarly research continues to focus on the human–nature interaction, as well as the heritage of Frederick Jackson Turner. His current project, a study of Turner's hometown of Portage, Wisconsin, sets out to combine and integrate the methods of environmental and social history.[4]

Cronon's career trajectory was already impressive before he published *Nature's Metropolis*, but the book pushed him into the upper echelons of the profession. After its publication, he chose to take up a chair at the University of Wisconsin despite Yale University's attempts to retain him. He served as the President of the American Historical Association in 2012 and remains one of the most respected historians in the United States, working in the same Midwestern region at the heart of *Nature's Metropolis*.

NOTES

1   William Cronon, *Changes in the Land: Indians, Colonists, and the Ecology of New England* (New York: Hill & Wang, 1983).

2   William Cronon, "The Trouble with Wilderness; or, Getting Back to the Wrong Nature," in *Uncommon Ground: Rethinking the Human Place in Nature*, ed. William Cronon (New York: W. W. Norton & Co., 1995), 69–99.

3   A rough sketch of the controversy, involving issues of political transparency and academic freedom, appears in the print version of the *New York Times* (March 28, 2011), A27.

4   See the "Current Projects" section of William Cronon's website: http://www.williamcronon.net/current_projects.htm.

SECTION 3
IMPACT

MODULE 9
THE FIRST RESPONSES

KEY POINTS

- There were two central objections to *Nature's Metropolis:* that the book employs outdated geographical models and fuzzy philosophical concepts; and that Cronon downgrades human agency (that is, the power of individuals to change the world through their actions) and political activity in explaining historical events.

- Otherwise, responses were largely positive. Widespread acceptance of both poststructuralism* and environmentalism meant the climate was hospitable to Cronon's approach.

- Cronon headed off criticism by developing his ideas further in subsequent essays; in particular, he clarified his intention to blur the lines dividing the natural environment and human action—or "first nature"* and "second nature" as he describes it in the book.

Criticism

William Cronon's *Nature's Metropolis: Chicago and the Great West* was greeted with widespread critical acclaim within the American historical profession and beyond. Historians hailed the book for its ambitious scope, detailed and thorough research and imaginative writing style. His supporters included the American environmental historian Richard White,* who embraced the book for putting environmental history* on the map.[1] In fact, most reviews were fantastically positive. And those historians critical of the book, such as Howard Rabinowitz,* generally came from an older generation attached to more conventional approaches to economic and political

> ❝ One of Cronon's numerous triumphs is to bring to the surface issues that concern virtually all environmental historians, and it would be slighting this landmark volume not to begin a serious dialogue within the field on the important issues Nature's Metropolis raises. ❞
>
> Richard White, Review of *Nature's Metropolis, Environmental History Review*

history, and a more robust view of human events.

Cronon's popularity stems in part from applying a fashionable postmodern* philosophy to the study of the city in the wilderness. Indeed, White applauds *Nature's Metropolis* for adopting postmodern analysis, an approach defined in part by a skepticism about the possibility of arriving at an objective truth, particularly because Cronon emphasizes the relationships *between* things rather than focusing on the things themselves.

White is not just pleased that Cronon's book boosted the emergence of environmental history—he even compares it (at something of a stretch) to Raymond Williams's classic *The Country and the City* to underline its significance.[2]

Yet the tendency of *Nature's Metropolis* to elevate the cause of nature over the cause of humanity remains the most persuasive and important criticism of the book. Those historians who still value human action as a primary force behind historical events include Rabinowitz,[3] Robert Rydell,*[4] Samuel Hays,*[5] and Peter Coclanis,*[6] all of whom reviewed the book.

As an example, Coclanis charges that Cronon romanticizes nature, presenting people as destroyers of tall grass prairies, bison herds and white pine forests. He condemns *Nature's Metropolis* as "a disturbingly anti-industrial, and ultimately misanthropic book."[7] Coclanis and

Rabinowitz both object to Cronon's self-referential and self-indulgent tone, and his supposedly profound (but in fact obvious and commonplace) claims about the dastardly, obscured acts of capital that he unveils.[8] These critics raise important questions about the Chicagoans involved in the creation of "the city in the garden":[9] namely, Cronon's neglect of their political motivations and the sense they made of the transformations they wrought.

Responses

In the years following *Nature's Metropolis*, William Cronon engaged the intellectual debate surrounding the book in two important ways. First, he took up the question of the environment and its place in environmental history. To this end, he answered his critics' charges that his conception of the natural world places it in a past, mythical golden age. Second, he addressed humanity's apparently destructive, depressing impact on the environment. Cronon neither refutes nor accepts the criticisms leveled against him. Rather, he restates his own position and further develops the ideas in *Nature's Metropolis*, clarifying methods and concepts he relied upon in the text.

Still, that doesn't mean Cronon ducked controversy. The article "The Trouble with Wilderness or, Getting Back to the Wrong Nature," develops the case Cronon initially outlined in *Nature's Metropolis*, charting the intertwining of human and natural worlds over the course of American history. It appeared in various places: as a roundtable debate focus in the first volume of *Environmental History*, in an edited collection and in the *New York Times*. In "Trouble," he argues that "wilderness" as we imagine it has no relationship to nature.[10] So Cronon asserts that his own concept of nature is not romantic* but located in historical change—and, as a result, must be understood through specific interactions with humans.   However, for environmentalists, Cronon's point was controversial and highly provocative. The article seemed to detract from arguments in favor of official protection and preservation of natural spaces. [11]

Cronon also tackled the question from the other side of the equation, stressing both the creative and the destructive impact as humanity interacts with and transforms nature. In "The Uses of Environmental History," Cronon underlines the historian's dual commitments to recognize the needs of the present and respect the integrity of the past. Cronon declares that the problem stems from people thinking they are outside of nature and avoiding responsibility for it as a result.[12]

Conflict and Consensus

In consultation with like-minded scholars from numerous fields, Cronon took part in a semester-long seminar to flesh out a new approach to nature. This culminated in the book *On Uncommon Ground*, which carried his wilderness essay alongside contributions from the historian Richard White and the historian and philosopher Carolyn Merchant* and others.[13]

The debate continues to focus on the relationship between humanity and nature, both in history and contemporary America. Responding to criticisms that his work places too much emphasis on the human-nature connection, Cronon points out that humans must be engaged because ultimately they threaten nature. He argues that environmentalists will lose their fight unless they listen to his insights about the interconnections between the two. Yet his argument remains unpersuasive—not only to environmentalists but also to his foremost academic critics, who continue to reject his anti-humanism and perceived smugness of tone.

The historian Samuel Hays questions Cronon's presentist use of history—that is, using the past to further his own environmental agenda. Hays is also impatient with the disconnection between Cronon's postmodern theoretical preoccupations and the experience of actual wilderness campaigners.[14] Yet though Cronon may never reach consensus or compromise with his detractors, he has certainly forced them to take stock of his ideas about the links between humanity and nature.

NOTES

1   Richard White, "Review of *Nature's Metropolis,*" *Environmental History Review* 16, no. 2 (1992): 85–91.

2   White, "Review of *Nature's Metropolis.*" Raymond Williams is widely held to be the founder of cultural studies. His book, *The Country and the City* (London: Chatto & Windus, 1973) no doubt informed Cronon's approach to some degree.

3   Howard N. Rabinowitz, "The New Western History Goes to Town, Or Don't Forget That Your Urban Hamburger Was Once a Rural Cow: A Review Essay," *Montana: The Magazine of Western History 43*, no. 2 (1993): 73–77.

4   Robert Rydell, "*Nature's Metropolis: Chicago and the Great West*. By William Cronon," Southwestern Historical Quarterly 97.1 (1993): 169–70.

5   Samuel P. Hays, "*Nature's Metropolis: Chicago and the Great West*. By William Cronon." Journal of American History 79.2 (1992): 612–13.

6   Peter A. Coclanis, "Urbs in Horto," *Reviews in American History 20*. 1 (1992), 14–20.

7   Coclanis, "Urbs in Horto," 18.

8   Coclanis, "Urbs in Horto"; Rabinowitz, "The New Western History Goes to Town."

9   Coclanis's review title "Urbs in Horto" translates directly as "the city in the garden" and it is the official motto of the city of Chicago.

10 William Cronon, "The Trouble with Wilderness or, Getting Back to the Wrong Nature," *Environmental History*, 1.1 (January 1996): 7–55 (Available to download here: http://www.williamcronon.net/writing/Trouble_with_Wilderness_Main.html), with comments by Samuel P. Hays, Michael P. Cohen, Thomas R. Dunlap, and a response by William Cronon; abridged version reprinted in the *New York Times Sunday Magazine* (August 13, 1995): 42–43.

11 Cronon, "The Trouble with Wilderness."

12 William Cronon, "The Uses of Environmental History," *Environmental History Review*, 17, no. 3 (1993): 1–22. Originally delivered as his Presidential Address to the American Society for Environmental History in 1993.

13 William Cronon (ed.), *Uncommon Ground: Rethinking the Human Place in Nature* (New York: W.W. Norton & Co., 1996).

14 Howard Rabinowitz describes Cronon's style as "self-indulgent, confessional, and at times preachy." See Howard Rabinowitz, "The New Western History Goes to Town," 75.

MODULE 10
THE EVOLVING DEBATE

KEY POINTS

- *Nature's Metropolis* opens the door to historical examination of natural and human phenomena in close interrelationship; the book erases the intellectual boundary between man and nature.

- *Nature's Metropolis* encourages historians to undertake interdisciplinary approaches in the study of the environment. Environmental history* falls into close relationship with urban and Western history and the history of technology.

- Some political and economic historians have resisted and challenged Cronon's approach. Essentially, those historians reject the book's philosophical assumptions because they prefer to view history as determined by human action, rather than large structures and processes.

Uses and Problems

Though William Cronon has not published any major scholarly works since *Nature's Metropolis: Chicago and the Great West,* he has collaborated with other environmental historians on two essay collections. He has also published a number of important articles that develop both his ideas about the environment and the philosophy and methodology of history.

These develop his ideas of nature as a cultural construction and history as something close to fictional narrative: the stories we tell.[1] Cronon was also founding editor of the Weyerhaeuser Environmental History series at the University of Washington Press, which states its mission as the casting of "new light on the ways that natural systems

> **❝** The primary objective of *Nature's Metropolis* is to reveal the unity of city and country that agrarian ideology has obscured. Such a task involves showing how the circulation of commodities simultaneously unites the city and country in ever tighter economic relationships while at the same time, through processes of abstraction, it obscures their connection. **❞**
>
> Robert D. Johnston, "Beyond 'The West': Regionalism, liberalism and the Evasion of Politics in the New Western History," in *Rethinking History*

affect human communities, the ways that people affect the environments of which they are a part, and the ways that different cultural conceptions of nature profoundly shape our sense of the world around us."

A number of contributors to the series are intellectually indebted to Cronon's work.[2] This is nearly a given, because *Nature's Metropolis* remains one of the defining, seminal texts in the new field of environmental history. According to Richard White,* its publication changed the status of environmental history from an interesting subfield to a central field of American history.[3] The impact was lasting and Nature's Metropolis continues to set a standard for environmental historians. In previous discussions of the environment, historians cast nature as passive, humanity as active.

Nature's Metropolis helped position the environment as an active element of human history. However, this is not a universally welcomed development; Robert D. Johnston* and Peter Coclanis* (political and economic historians respectively) object to Cronon's downgrading of human agency. Johnston, for instance, argues that Cronon's approach misses "a sense that conflicts over power, resources, and ideology can actually transform the structures that govern people's economic and cultural lives—that 'the socialization of conflict' ... can actually lead anywhere beyond the fundamental liberal pattern of individual profit-maximization and group interest-based strife."[4] Coclanis cites the book's "imbalance, and its author's lack of empathy with man, his cities and his desire for material gain."[5] Human activity is only acknowledged where it harms the environment.

Schools of Thought

While there is no Cronon school of thought per se, environmental historians have adopted many of his concepts. In that context, Cronon ranks as a leading figure in environmental history alongside other key thinkers: Richard White, Carolyn Merchant,* and Donald Worster.* These historians have brought the natural world into the story of American history and, though differences exist among them, they largely share a critical understanding of how American civilization transformed the natural environment. Few if any authors have replicated Cronon's magisterial achievement, but many academics—including Cronon's own graduate students—have translated their admiration into works of their own.[6]

Cronon also numbers among the New Western historians to reinvent study of the American West. While *Nature's Metropolis* has influenced numerous fields, the book's methodology and philosophical approach have been especially embraced by the historical profession. Clearly, its sophistication and creative mix of disciplines have strengthened the authority of poststructuralist* approaches to history.

In Current Scholarship

Environmental historians have inserted Cronon's insights into American history in imaginative ways. For example, Robert Keiter* examines the history of American national parks; James Morton Turner* traces the history of the American wilderness ideal; and Mark Fiege* reimagines icons of American history through the lens of nature's influence.[7] There are also numerous innovations in environmental history beyond the American border that bear the mark of Cronon's influence.[8]

However, as Cronon himself notes, environmental history still promotes a depressing narrative of decline that he claims to oppose and seeks to counteract.[9] Cronon conceives man and nature in a mutually reinforcing relationship. In somewhat similar fashion, many environmental historians understand the environment as an arena for human action. Sometimes, that is for good—but usually for ill.

Cronon's use of poststructual theory has probably wielded most influence over current thinking about the environment. The recurring myth of a natural world untainted by human touch or exploitation has dominated past historical discussions. Led by Cronon, environmental historians continue to deconstruct the nature/culture opposition; the latter Cronon pinpoints as capital.

Although Cronon objects to either incumbent politicians or environmental reformers trying to influence his research agenda to advance narrow and immediate policy concerns he is keen to utilize the power and influence of his work to help shape policy.[10] He appeared in the influential documentary-maker Ken Burns'* pro-conservationist documentary about America's National Parks.[11]

Cronon's personal website lists the many ways in which he actively works with environmental and conservationist organizations— though he also hopes to convince them of the folly of trying to preserve a mythical "wilderness."[12] His environmentalism is, rather, more mediated and pragmatic. Though he aims to protect the natural environment, he sees it as inextricably linked to human existence and so does not treat nature or society as separate.

Despite some resistance, Cronon's approach has begun to penetrate the environmental movement and public policy objectives. In time, his actions may well change the histories future environmental historians write.

NOTES

1   William Cronon, "The Uses of Environmental History," *Environmental History Review*, 17, no. 3 (1993): 1–22; Cronon, "The Trouble with Wilderness or, Getting Back to the Wrong Nature," *Environmental History*, 1.1 (January 1996): 7–55; Cronon, "A Place for Stories: Nature, History, and Narrative," *Journal of American History* 78:4 (March, 1992), 1347–76.

2   The series list is available here: http://www.washington.edu/uwpress/books/series/Seriesweyerenv.html.

3   Richard White, "Review of Nature's Metropolis," *Environmental History Review* 16.2 (1992), 85.

4   Robert D. Johnston, "Beyond 'The West': Regionalism, Liberalism and the Evasion of Politics in the New Western History," *Rethinking History* Vol. 2.2 (1998), 241.

5   Peter Coclanis, "Urbs in Horto," *Reviews in American History* 20.1 (1992), 16.

6   Cronon lists his students and former students, including their publications and current positions, on his website: http://www.williamcronon.net/students.htm.

7   Robert B. Keiter, To Conserve Unimpaired: *The Evolution of the National Park Idea* (Washington, DC: Island Press, 2013); James Morton Turner, *The Promise of Wilderness* (Seattle: University of Washington Press, 2012); Mark Fiege, *Republic of Nature* (Seattle: University of Washington Press, 2012).

8   See, for example, Brett L. Walker's *The Lost Wolves of Japan* (Seattle: University of Washington Press, 2008), which appeared in the series edited by Cronon.

9   Cronon, "The Uses of Environmental History."

10 Cronon, "The Uses of Environmental History."

11 Ken Burns, *The National Parks*: America's Best Idea is a PBS film. It is hosted on an interactive website: www.pbs.org/nationalparks/, accessed September 23, 2013.

12 Cronon's environmental activism is substantial. A full list of the organizations with which he is involved is available on his political blog at http://www.williamcronon.net/land_conservation.htm, accessed July 10, 2015.

MODULE 11
IMPACT AND INFLUENCE TODAY

KEY POINTS

* *Nature's Metropolis* remains highly regarded and has withstood most of the critical responses it received.

* The book still challenges historians to reconsider the relationship between humanity and nature; to rethink the interactions between rural and urban locations; and to reframe the understanding of human events in history.

* Environmental historians have taken on the challenge to move past oppositional divisions between nature and humanity, as well as city and countryside. Yet political and economic historians resist and attempt to downplay human agency and political action as drivers of historical change.

Position

Since *Nature's Metropolis: Chicago and the Great West*, William Cronon has been at the forefront of environmental history* and its expansion, editing a series of books that take up many of the themes he flagged as important.[1] Few historians have confronted the issue of human–natural encounters in such an innovative manner as Cronon in *Nature's Metropolis*, but some—including many contributors to his edited series—have followed his lead. As a result, the natural environment now enters into historical discussions once seen as purely social or cultural.

Cronon interrogates the borders between things rather than the things themselves and thus gives added impetus toward poststructuralist* modes of history writing. This trend has encouraged many historians to probe other areas in similar ways, considering the

> ❝ This was an excellent book when it was first
> published nearly twenty years ago, and it ... has certainly
> held up well since then, its continued popularity for
> classroom assignment and the frequency of its citation
> being only two of several factors attesting to its classic
> status. Whether one is a historian of technology or
> the environment, or an economic or urban or western
> historian, there is still much to ponder in this geographic
> mapping of nineteenth-century Chicago and its wide-
> reaching hinterland. ❞
>
> Stephen H. Cutliffe, "Travels in and Out of Town: William Cronon's *Nature's Metropolis,*" *Technology and Culture*

fluid relationships between things and groups of people—and especially between nations—by examining the "borderlands" between them.[2]

Though Cronon conceives of himself as both an urban historian and an environmental historian, Nature's Metropolis has not been so influential in the first field as in the second; a 2010 survey found that urban historians, when they dealt with the natural world, continued to offer a narrative of humans as agents of destruction and pollution.[3]

Few have picked up Cronon's distinction between "first" nature* and "second" nature, perhaps because Cronon's book left these concepts vague and ill defined.[4] Some urban historians, however, are not only adopting more sophisticated approaches but also paying homage to Cronon as they do so; a collection of essays about the City of Philadelphia published in 2012, for example, is titled *Nature's Entrepôt*—both a reference to the city's role as a trading port and a direct tribute to *Nature's Metropolis*.[5]

Interaction

American historians continue to hold *Nature's Metropolis* in high regard. It is often found on college reading lists and is seen as contributing to several fields of history. Since the book's release, Cronon has worked inside and outside academia to defend his core argument: that it is impossible to protect pristine, untouched nature from the reach of human involvement. Granted, this argument has proven quite controversial. But many historians have most actively embraced Cronon's view of capitalism* as the active engine that drives historical change.

Cronon turns historical thinking on its head by contending that no meaningful distinction exists between man and nature. He contends that nature is man-made, humans natural. Few historians meet his challenge directly by defending human action as the most crucial factor, but many continue to uphold a structural wall between humanity and the environment, or remain opposed to Cronon's undermining of the distinctions between the city and countryside. This might be because cities and rural farms still exist as separate sites with different social, economic, and cultural dynamics. Nevertheless, other historians who back poststructural theories continue to champion Cronon's argument that "what we call city" and "what we call countryside" contain more differences in the words that signify them than in the historical reality. Indeed poststructuralism sees any such "reality" as the historian's creation.

The Continuing Debate

Though some scholars still wrestle with Cronon's book, most of the continuing controversy takes place outside academia. The book is largely accepted as a gateway to understanding Western and environmental history—while dissenters in urban history, for example, ignore it, bypass it, or rarely challenge it. Taking it on is an intimidating task: *Nature's Metropolis* is already a classic both within environmental history and in the broader historical field.

That established, Cronon has by no means closed the door on debate, or even removed himself from it. On the one hand, many historians tip the scale towards humans and their activity; on the other, environmentalists tip it back to nature and the need to protect pristine, unexploited "wilderness" from human encroachments. Inserting himself in the middle, Cronon suggests no real conflict of interest exists because there is no humanity without nature and no nature without humanity. Yet his argument that there can be no unspoiled wilderness has angered campaigners who charge him with playing both sides of the field. They accuse him of displaying the same arrogant humanism his work purports to challenge.

A small group of historians continue to suggest that Cronon's analysis in *Nature's Metropolis* contains serious flaws. Indeed, the historian Robert Johnston* suggests that Cronon and other historians of the New Western* school replicate errors made by the old Western history by essentializing* the West (that is, they regard it as having some innate quality, or "essence," outside of the social, ideological, or intellectual frames of reference we use to define things). Johnston charges that Cronon continues elements of mythology about the symbolic significance of "the West" in order to give Western history a greater significance within the historical profession.[6]

Moreover, within the realm of environmental history, in which Cronon remains widely admired and cited, a junior historian argues against unthinking endorsements. Joshua MacFadyen* suggests "scholars do scholarship a disservice when we overquote, overcite or, let's face it, simply namedrop" and that "environmental historians have been doing William Cronon a disservice in recent years by referring to rather than responding to his work."[7] Perhaps some scope for fresh debate within academia is opening up—a prospect that Cronon will surely welcome.

NOTES

1   Cronon is the series editor of the Weyerhaeuser Environmental Book Series and writes forewords to all books in the series. He has also edited many books in the Lamar Series in Western History for Yale University Press.

2   For an authoritative guide to this shift, see Akira Iriye, *Global and Transnational History: The Past, Present, and Future* (New York: Palgrave Pivot, 2012).

3   Martin V. Melosi, "Humans, Cities, and Nature: How do Cities Fit in the Material World?," *Journal of Urban History* 36, no. 1 (2010): 3–21.

4   In his otherwise admiring review of Cronon's book, Richard White states that the use of the terms "first" and "second" nature are "infelicitous" and "conceptually confusing." See *Environmental History Review* 16, no. 2 (1992): 90.

5   Brian C. Black, Michael J. Chiarappa, eds. *Nature's Entrepôt: Philadelphia's Urban Sphere and Its Environmental Thresholds* (Pittsburgh: University of Pittsburgh Press, 2012).

6   Robert D. Johnston, "Beyond 'The West': Regionalism, Liberalism, and the Evasion of Politics in the New Western History," *Rethinking History* 2, no. 2 (1998): 239–77.

7   Joshua MacFadyen, "What We Talk About When We Talk About William Cronon," accessed November 1, 2013, http://niche-canada.org/node/10583.

MODULE 12
WHERE NEXT?

KEY POINTS

- The scholarly impact of *Nature's Metropolis* can be seen as historians embrace the book's poststructural* analytical approach. They also continue Cronon's investigation into the humanity-nature relationship, which has created real-world impact as well.

- As a foundational text in the field, *Nature's Metropolis* will continue to influence environmental history* and encourage the naturalization of capitalist* relations in particular.

- The book is also a seminal work in Western history, reinvigorating the field while giving greater intellectual weight to environmental history. Cronon's ability to synthesize, his willingness to experiment with new concepts, and his deep research mean the book has rarely been equaled since its publication.

Potential

Given its dominance in environmental history, William Cronon's *Nature's Metropolis*: Chicago and the Great West is likely to retain its influence for some time to come. In other fields, where historians have articulated frustration alongside their admiration for the book, it is easier to see it becoming more marginal. Still it is likely that a new generation of historians will tackle the book in critical and creative ways so that its core ideas might further develop.[1]

It is also possible that younger historians will refer to Cronon's work while pursuing their own agendas.

The recent trend that sets American history on the world stage as a

> ❝ Writing urban environmental history, then, is less about reconciling contradictions than it is about revealing the prehistoric foundations our Faustian culture cannot escape as it forever seeks to build a better world. ❞
>
> Bruce Stephenson, "Urban Environmental History: the Essence of a Contradiction," *Journal of Urban History*

part of the globalization* story might work to reduce the book's influence. After all, *Nature's Metropolis* deals with a city and region within a nation—all with a narrow time frame—and thus has little reference to the world outside those bounds. Yet the opposite may hold true: that globalization might actually provide fresh opportunities to expand Cronon's interpretive tools, since capitalism* and its logic easily apply to global history through the twenty-first century. Moreover, Cronon's environmental focus also means he is involved in the seemingly opposed but actually connected trend of focusing on local communities. Cronon is currently working on a local history of Portage, Wisconsin, Frederick Jackson Turner's hometown.

Future Directions

A second generation of scholars within the relatively new field of environmental history is emerging and recent works show the influence of Cronon's thinking in Nature's Metropolis. Indeed, many of these young scholars are either Cronon's former students or else authors whose first monographs have been published in his edited series of books.[2]

Their general consensus is that Cronon's work, both in *Changes in the Land* and *Nature's Metropolis*, represent hallowed foundational texts for their field. They either seek to emulate Cronon or provide building-block case studies to bolster aspects of environmental history that he and leading scholars have demarcated. The key debates in US environmental history focus on three central questions Cronon outlines in the courses he teaches:

- how human activities in the past have depended on, and interacted with, the natural world and vice versa
- the way American attitudes toward nature have shifted across the nation's history
- how human attitudes and activities, including political and reform activities, have reshaped the American landscape.

This second generation of environmental historians has embraced Cronon's understanding of capitalism's negative impact on the natural environment. Yet while many of their texts recount the environmental costs of capitalist expansion, they downplay complementary, positive ideas about the creative opportunities capitalist expansion produces. Cronon himself suggests the dramatic creativity of capitalism—for example, in his vivid descriptions of the "golden stream" that capital made from sacks of wheat—even if this is implicit rather than dominant in his analysis.[3] Cronon also expresses surprise that his students often come away from his courses with a rather depressed air about the future of humanity and the planet.[4]

Outside the classroom, *Nature's Metropolis* has prompted greater interest in the ways technology and nature interrelate. Scholarly conferences, journals, websites, and monographs have explored the intersecting histories of "nature and technology." Indeed, the publication of Nature's Metropolis helped spur the establishment of Envirotech, a special interest group with links to the Society for the History of Technology and the American Society for Environmental History. Envirotech hosts its own website, publishes a bi-annual newsletter and organizes professional events.[5] Its scholarship points to the "illusory boundary" between human beings—especially their technology—and the natural world.[6]

Many historians, and environmental historians in particular, have embraced Cronon's use of poststructuralist theory. They often quote him directly and approvingly to justify their adoption of poststructuralist ideas, such as the social construction of nature or the false duality in the natural–human split. Perhaps the theory will need no justification in years to come; as American historian William Graebner* recently noted, "[we] are all poststructuralists" now.

Summary

William Cronon's *Nature's Metropolis* deserves, and has received, special attention from the historical profession—and the reasons are many. Cronon uses an innovative, interdisciplinary approach, sophisticated application of theory, and a deep evidence base, all delivered in elegant prose. The book gives a new field of enquiry—environmental history—an unprecedented level of significance, cementing its importance among subfields of American history.

Although the book's originality is evident on many levels, the text also builds on the arguments of past scholarship. It succeeds by combining approaches from environmental, urban, and Western history, along with the disciplines of geography and economics. What's more, its argument is rich and multilayered, taking concrete developments and teasing out their abstract meaning and significance.

Cronon, however, illustrates the abstract through the concrete: something as simple as tracing the changes in transporting a sack of wheat to market. Armed with poststructural theory, Cronon deconstructs* the difference between town and country and between human and nonhuman influences on history. This theoretical approach gives the book added status among historians.

Cronon shows how urban and rural locations intertwine so closely that any distinctions between them are in fact arbitrary. And his overarching thesis promotes capitalist social relations as the dynamo behind social and economic change, affecting both people and their environment in mostly negative ways. Chicagoans and Midwestern farmers become the tools of capitalism's inner logic for destroying the natural environment.

This final point, distressing as it may seem, reflects Cronon's reading of the past—and not his predictions for the future. Remember: this visionary historian also sees capitalism as a potentially positive force. And in the current era of globalization, it's entirely possible that *Nature's Metropolis* will revolutionize how politicians and environmentalists think about world, just as it shook up the world of history itself.

NOTES

1   Josh MacFadyen, "What We Talk About When We Talk About William Cronon," accessed September 23, 2013 http://niche-canada.org/node/10583.

2   Cronon edited and wrote prefaces for all of the books in the Weyerhaeuser Environmental Book series, accessed September 23, 2013, http://www.washington.edu/uwpress/books/series/Seriesweyerenv.html.

3   See William Cronon, *Nature's Metropolis: Chicago and the Great West* (New York: W. W. Norton& Co., 1992), 109–20.

4   William Cronon, "The Uses of Environmental History," *Environmental History Review*, 17, no. 3 (1993): 1–22.

5   See Envirotech website, accessed July 10, 2015, http://www.envirotechweb.org.

6   Stephen H. Cutliffe, "Travels In and Out of Town: William Cronon's *Nature's Metropolis,*" *Technology and Culture* Vol. 51.3 (July 2010), 728.

GLOSSARY

GLOSSARY OF TERMS

Annales school: a group of French structuralist historians who worked on or wrote for the influential historical journal Annales d'Histoire Economique et Sociale.

Anthropomorphism: a tendency to attribute human characteristics to a nonhuman entity such as an animal or nature.

Capitalism: a system of political economy characterized by commodity exchange through a market mechanism guided by the primary aim of making profit.

Capitalist: an individual who owns and operates the productive machinery of a company. Capitalist manufacturers then work with merchants to distribute goods and seek to maximize profit through the market mechanism of commodity exchange.

Capitalist market: the working mechanism through which goods are distributed and money is exchanged within a capitalist system of political economy. Manufacturers and merchants seek to maximize profit through it.

Central place theory: a geographical theory developed by German geographer Walter Christaller that explains the organization of different types of settlements in an urban system. For Christaller, cities function as "central places" within regions and provided essential products and services to surrounding areas.

Chicago Board of Trade: established in 1848, the world's oldest futures and options exchange market. It is still located in downtown Chicago.

Commodity fetishism: a way of thinking about commodities that misunderstands and wrongly elevates their significance. It replaces social relationships between people with economic relationships between the products that they trade. It mistakes the subjective, abstract aspects of economic value for objective, real things with intrinsic value. Capital, as Cronon points out, is not a thing but a relationship.

Declensionist: Declensionist narratives tell pessimistic stories of degeneration, failure, decline, loss, and decay.

Deconstruction: a concept flowing from the poststructuralist theory associated with the philosopher Jacques Derrida's foundational text, Of Grammatology (1967), which first appeared in English translation in 1976 and has been influential in Western thought ever since. It assumes that differences between things are largely, if not wholly, linguistically constructed. Cronon's analysis seeks to deconstruct the binary oppositions presented in conventional understandings of city and countryside.

Determinism: approach that understands human activity as limited, or determined, by external forces, usually economic or environmental.

Dust bowl: a region subject to drought where, as a result of the loss or absence of plant cover, the wind has eroded the soil and made the land unproductive; hence, any region that is arid or unproductive. In US history, the term is often associated with the dust storms that occurred in Oklahoma, Texas, Kansas, and other Western states in the 1930s.

Elevator (grain): a facility, usually mechanized, for sorting and storing grain.

Environmental history: the study of the history of human action on the environment.

Essentialism: the practice of considering something—such as a geographical region—as having an innate, unchanging inner essence.

First nature: in Cronon's usage, an abundant, unspoiled, pristine nature untouched by human activity; second nature, by contrast, is transformed by human activity.

Frontier thesis: Frederick Jackson Turner's important "frontier thesis" stressed the evolutionary impact that taming wilderness had on the American character. He argued that it was direct experience of the frontier rather than any European heritage that molded Americans' attachment to democracy, equality, and individualism.

Globalization: the process of global interaction, exchange, and integration of views, products, ideas, and other aspects of culture.

Great Depression: a worldwide economic depression that took place in the 1930s, following the Wall Street Crash of 1929. It had a dramatic and transformative impact on the politics and economy of many nations, including the United States.

Historicism: Historicism emphasizes the importance of context—both in time and place—for understanding the meaning of historical events. Historicism is usually understood as a form of relativism: that is, there is nothing real about the object of enquiry; the past only exists in human perceptions of it.

Industrial location theory: approach that seeks to explain why particular companies choose to locate where they do. It usually attributes strategic location to ease of access to transportation at both ends of the productive process. Cronon neglects this theory, preferring to emphasize Johann Heinrich von Thünen's argument that agricultural practices were determined by the value of the product and the cost of transporting it to town.

Industrialization: the process of mechanizing labor, and a movement away from an economy based on agriculture. The process of industrialization generally changes a landscape.

Isolated state theory: In his classic study The Isolated State (1826), von Thünen argued that agricultural practices would be determined by the value of the product and the cost of transporting it to a central city. His theory states that heavy and perishable goods such as dairy produce will be farmed close to town while livestock will be further away.

Labor theory of value: a theory stating that the value inherent in a commodity is wholly derived from the labor contained within it—that is, the human labor used to produce it. Cronon disputes the theory by emphasizing the value inherent in "first nature."

Misanthropy: the general distrust of or disdain for the human species.

New Social history: New Social historians sought to use social scientific analysis as part of their discipline and employed, in particular, statistical analyses of large population groups to highlight broad social trends. Working in the 1960s and 1970s, and influenced by the New Left they focused on history "from below" (concentrating on overlooked individuals and communities rather than that directed by elites). New Western history followed a similar pattern a decade later, but in a regional context.

New Western history: a regional manifestation of the New Social history that emerged in the 1980s. Both approaches represented a critique of older "top-down" histories and focused on previously overlooked groups at the bottom of the social hierarchy. They dealt with issues of race, class, gender, and environment in the trans-Mississippi West. Historians Patricia Nelson Limerick, Richard White, William Cronon, and Donald Worster are most associated with the New Western History.

Nietzscheanism: Based on the work of Frederick Nietzsche (1844–1900), Nietzschean philosophy is usually associated with fatalism, nihilism, and a rejection of both religious and humanistic attempts to create meaning.

Occupy movement: a global protest movement for social justice. The movement began in Zuccotti Park, New York City, as "Occupy Wall Street" on September 17, 2011. Occupy membership is concentrated in Western nations but its campaigns target global economic inequalities.

Postmodernism: a broad term referring to a philosophical outlook that takes a skeptical, and often ironic, approach to truth claims.

Poststructuralism: theory that refers to the deconstruction of either-or oppositions that structuralist thinkers rely upon to understand social and linguistic systems.

Presentism: a mode of historical analysis in which present-day ideas, agendas, or perspectives are introduced into depictions or interpretations of the past.

Revisionism: refers to the challenge by one generation of historians to the previous generation's orthodox interpretations. It is sometimes used negatively but not always since each successive generation tends to revise the orthodoxies of the last.

Romanticism: an artistic and intellectual movement dominant in the nineteenth century that rejected the scientific rationalization of nature. It emphasized and encouraged an emotional, rather than rational, response to and association with natural phenomena.

Teleology: an explanation of change that depends upon a thing's final end goal, purpose or reason. It suggests a built-in fate. Turner's frontier thesis is held to be teleological because it sees history as tending inevitably towards a final end, as a march of human progress.

Urban boosters: Urban boosters are usually city officials or businessmen with an interest in the success of a city who seek to raise the estimation and status of the city by positive public praise.

Whig History: the approach to history that reads the past as an inexorable and inevitable march of progress from ignorance and want to enlightenment and plenty in the present. Usually applied as a pejorative term. For Cronon's muted usage, see William Cronon, "Two Cheers for the Whig Interpretation of History," Perspectives on History (September 2012).

Wisconsin idea: approach that originated in the early twentieth century as a way of connecting the intellectual output of universities with the social and political needs of the state. Cronon's home institution, the University of Wisconsin, led this public-spirited attempt to inform public policy with thorough evidence-based scientific and social scientific research.

PEOPLE MENTIONED IN THE TEXT

Ken Burns (b. 1953) is an American director and award-winning documentary filmmaker. His historical documentaries, including *The Civil War* and *Jazz*, have won many accolades, honors, and awards.

Rachel Carson (1907–64) was an American marine biologist and nature writer whose work is widely credited with launching the modern environmentalist movement. Her popular book *Silent Spring* (1962) highlighted the detrimental effect of the use of pesticides, specifically DDT, on birds, animals, and humans.

Peter A. Coclanis (b. 1952) is an American historian specializing in economic and business history. He is Albert Ray Newsome Distinguished Professor and Director of the Global Research Institute at the University of North Carolina, Chapel Hill.

Dr. E. David Cronon (1924–2006) was an American historian. The father of historian William Cronon, he served as chair of the History department at the University of Wisconsin and later became dean of the College of Letters and Science.

Mike Davis (b. 1946) is an American writer, political activist, urban theorist, and historian. He is a distinguished professor in the Department of Creative Writing at the University of California, Riverside, and an editor of the *New Left Review*.

John Mack Faragher is Arthur Unobskey Professor of History, Professor of American Studies, and director of the Howard R. Lamar Center for the Study of Frontiers and Borders at Yale University. He is a pioneer in the field of the New Western History.

Mark Fiege is an American historian of the environment and the American West. He is William E. Morgan Professor of Liberal Arts at Colorado State University. Fiege is the author of Irrigated Eden: The *Making of an Agricultural Landscape in the American West* (1999) and The *Republic of Nature* (2011), which contains a foreword by William Cronon.

William Graebner is an American historian. He is currently professor of history at the State University of New York, College at Fredonia.

Samuel P. Hays is an American historian specializing in the history of environmental policy. He is Distinguished Service Professor of History Emeritus, University of Pittsburgh.

Robinson Jeffers (1887–1962) was an American poet whose poems gained popularity during the interwar period. They addressed themes relating to the natural environment—especially the Californian coast—and were loaded with Nietzschean philosophy.

Robert D. Johnston is professor of history and director of teaching of history program, Department of History, University of Illinois at Chicago and author of *The Radical Middle Class: Populist Democracy and The Question of Capitalism in Progressive Era Portland, Oregon.*

Robert B. Keiter is an American legal scholar. He is Wallace Stegner Professor of Law at the University of Utah. His numerous publications examine the history of environmental law and public lands policy; his most recent book is *To Conserve Unimpaired: The Evolution of the National Park Idea* (2013).

Howard R. Lamar is Sterling Professor Emeritus of History, former president of Yale University and editor of *The New Encyclopedia of the American West*. He is a pioneer in the field of the New Western History.

Patricia Nelson Limerick began her career at Yale and then moved out West. She is currently professor of history, and faculty director of the Center of the American West, at the University of Colorado at Boulder. She is best known for her classic book, *The Legacy of Conquest: The Unbroken Past of the American West*.

Joshua MacFadyen is a Canadian environmental and digital historian. He is a postdoctoral fellow in history at the University of Saskatchewan and a Project Director at the Network in Canadian History and Environment.

Karl Marx (1818–83) was a German political economist. A revolutionary thinker, his writings encouraged and heralded the creation of communist societies around the world, particularly in Soviet Russia. His followers are known as Marxists.

Carolyn Merchant (b. 1936) is am American philosopher and historian. She is professor of environmental history, philosophy, and ethics at the University of California, Berkeley. Her most important book is *The Death of Nature: Women, Ecology, and the Scientific Revolution*.

Howard N. Rabinowitz (1942–98) was an American historian specializing in urban history and the history of race relations in the US. He was professor of history at the University of New Mexico.

Robert Rydell is an American historian specializing in US intellectual and cultural history. He is Michael P. Malone Professor of History at Montana State University.

Frederick Jackson Turner (1861–1932) was an American historian closely associated with the Progressive school of US history. His "frontier thesis" located the origin of the modern democratic character in the free and fluid condition of the American frontier. His work in western history had, and continues to have, an enormous impact on historical scholarship.

James Morton Turner is an American historian of climate, the environment and science & technology. He is associate professor of environmental studies at Wellesley College and author of *The Promise of Wilderness* (2012).

Johann Heinrich von Thünen (1783–1850) was a German landowning farmer and economist. He created an innovative analytical model of spatial economics and economic geography that became highly influential among both economists and geographers.

Richard White (b. 1947) is an American historian, specifically of environmental history and the US West. He is currently the Margaret Byrne Professor of American History at Stanford University; a faculty co-director of the Bill Lane Center for the American West; and a former president of the Organization of American Historians.

Raymond Williams (1921–88) was a British cultural critic, novelist, and academic who taught at both Oxford and Cambridge universities. He was a significant figure in the New Left. In addition to *The Country and the City* (1973), major works included *Culture and Society* (1958).

Donald Worster (b. 1941) is an American historian who was professor of American history at the University of Kansas. He was a key figure in the establishment of environmental history and his numerous works in environmental history include *Nature's Economy: A History of Ecological Ideas and Dust Bowl: the Southern Plains in the 1930s.*

WORKS CITED

WORKS CITED

Black, Brian C. and Michael J. Chiarappa, eds. *Nature's Entrepôt: Philadelphia's Urban Sphere and Its Environmental Thresholds*. Pittsburgh: University of Pittsburgh Press, 2012.

Carson, Rachel. *Silent Spring*. Boston: Houghton Mifflin, 1962.

Coclanis, Peter. "Urbs in Horto." *Reviews in American History* 20, no. 1 (1992): 14–20.

Cronon, William. *Changes in the Land: Indians, Colonists, and the Ecology of New England*. New York: Hill & Wang, 1983.

___. *Nature's Metropolis: Chicago and the Great West*. New York: W.W. Norton & Co., 1992.

___. "A Place for Stories: Nature, History, and Narrative." *Journal of American History* 78:4 (March, 1992): 1347–76.

___. "Revisiting the Vanishing Frontier: The Legacy of Frederick Jackson Turner." *Western Historical Quarterly* 18, no. 2 (April, 1987): 157–76.

___. "The Uses of Environmental History." *Environmental History Review*, 17, no. 3 (Fall 1993): 1–22.

___. "The Trouble with Wilderness; or, Getting Back to the Wrong Nature." In *Uncommon Ground: Rethinking the Human Place in Nature*, edited by William Cronon, 69–91. New York: W. W. Norton & Co., 1995.

Cutliffe, Stephen H. "Travels in and Out of Town: William Cronon's *Nature's Metropolis.*" *Technology and Culture* Vol. 51, no. 3 (July, 2010): 728–37.

Davis, Mike. Ecology of Fear: *Los Angeles and the Imagination of Disaster*. London: Vintage Books, 1999.

Derrida, Jacques. *Of Grammatology*. Paris: Les Éditions de Minuit, 1967.

Fiege, Mark. *Republic of Nature*. Seattle: University of Washington Press, 2012.

Hays, Samuel P. *Conservation and the Gospel of Efficiency: The Progressive Conservation Movement*, 1890–1920. Cambridge, Mass.: Harvard University Press, 1959.

___. "*Nature's Metropolis: Chicago and the Great West. By William Cronon.*" *Journal of American History* 79.2 (1992): 612–13.

Iriye, Akira. *Global and Transnational History: The Past, Present, and Future*. New York: Palgrave Pivot, 2012.

Johnston, Robert D. "Beyond 'The West': Regionalism, Liberalism and the Evasion of Politics in the New Western History." *Rethinking History* Vol. 2.2 (1998): 239–77.

Keiter, Robert B. To Conserve Unimpaired: *The Evolution of the National Park Idea*. Washington, D.C.: Island Press, 2013.

Lamar, Howard R, ed. *The New Encyclopedia of the American West*. New Haven: Yale University Press, 1998.

Limerick, Patricia Nelson. *The Legacy of Conquest: The Unbroken Past of the American West*. New York: W.W. Norton & Co., 1987.

MacEachern, Alan. "What We Talk About When We Talk About William Cronon." Network in Canadian History and Environment, February 4, 2013. Accessed 8 July, 2015, http://niche-canada.org/2013/02/04/what-we-talk-about-when-we-talk-about-william-cronon/.

Melosi, Martin V., "Humans, Cities, and Nature: How do Cities Fit in the Material World?" *Journal of Urban History 36*, no.1 (2010): 3–21.

Merchant, Carolyn. *The Death of Nature: Women, Ecology, and the Scientific Revolution*. San Francisco: Harper & Row, 1980.

Nash, Roderick. *Wilderness and the American Mind*. New Haven: Yale University Press, 1967.

Page, Brian, and Richard Walker. "*Nature's Metropolis*: The Ghost Dance of Christaller and von Thünen." *Antipode* 26.2 (1994): 152–62.

Rabinowitz, Howard. "The New Western History Goes to Town, Or Don't Forget That Your Urban Hamburger Was Once a Rural Cow: A Review Essay." *Montana: The Magazine of Western History* 43, no. 2 (1993): 73–77.

Rydell, Robert W. "Nature's Metropolis: Chicago and the Great West. By William Cronon." *Southwestern Historical Quarterly* 97.1 (1993): 169–70.

Stephenson, Bruce. "Urban Environmental History: The Essence of a Contradiction." *Journal of Urban History* 31 (September 2005): 887–98.

Turner, Frederick Jackson. "The Significance of the Frontier in American History." *Proceedings of the State Historical Society of Wisconsin* (December 14, 1893): 199–227.

Turner, James Morton. *The Promise of Wilderness*. Seattle: University of Washington Press, 2012.

Walker, Brett L. *The Lost Wolves of Japan*. Seattle: University of Washington Press, 2008.

Walker, Richard A. *The Country in the City: The Greening of the San Francisco Bay Area*. Seattle: University of Washington Press, 2008.

White, Richard. "American Environmental History: The Development of a New Historical Field." *Pacific Historical Review* 54, no. 3 (August, 1985): 297–335.

___. *The Middle Ground: Indians, Empires, and Republics in the Great Lakes Region*, 1650–1815. Cambridge: Cambridge University Press, 1991.

___. *Railroaded: The Transcontinentals and the Making of Modern America*. New York: W.W. Norton & Co., 2012.

___. "*Nature's Metropolis: Chicago and the Great West, 1848–1893 by William Cronon.*" *Environmental History Review* 16.2 (Summer, 1992): 85–91.

Williams, Raymond. *The Country and the City*. London: Chatto & Windus, 1973.

Worster, Donald. *Dust Bowl: The Southern Plains in the 1930s*. Oxford: Oxford University Press, 1979.

___. *Nature's Economy: A History of Ecological Ideas*. Cambridge: Cambridge University Press, 2nd ed., 1994.

THE MACAT LIBRARY
BY DISCIPLINE

AFRICANA STUDIES

Chinua Achebe's *An Image of Africa: Racism in Conrad's Heart of Darkness*
W. E. B. Du Bois's *The Souls of Black Folk*
Zora Neale Huston's *Characteristics of Negro Expression*
Martin Luther King Jr's *Why We Can't Wait*
Toni Morrison's *Playing in the Dark: Whiteness in the American Literary Imagination*

ANTHROPOLOGY

Arjun Appadurai's *Modernity at Large: Cultural Dimensions of Globalisation*
Philippe Ariès's *Centuries of Childhood*
Franz Boas's *Race, Language and Culture*
Kim Chan & Renée Mauborgne's *Blue Ocean Strategy*
Jared Diamond's *Guns, Germs & Steel: the Fate of Human Societies*
Jared Diamond's *Collapse: How Societies Choose to Fail or Survive*
E. E. Evans-Pritchard's *Witchcraft, Oracles and Magic Among the Azande*
James Ferguson's *The Anti-Politics Machine*
Clifford Geertz's *The Interpretation of Cultures*
David Graeber's *Debt: the First 5000 Years*
Karen Ho's *Liquidated: An Ethnography of Wall Street*
Geert Hofstede's *Culture's Consequences: Comparing Values, Behaviors, Institutes and Organizations across Nations*
Claude Lévi-Strauss's *Structural Anthropology*
Jay Macleod's *Ain't No Makin' It: Aspirations and Attainment in a Low-Income Neighborhood*
Saba Mahmood's *The Politics of Piety: The Islamic Revival and the Feminist Subject*
Marcel Mauss's *The Gift*

BUSINESS

Jean Lave & Etienne Wenger's *Situated Learning*
Theodore Levitt's *Marketing Myopia*
Burton G. Malkiel's *A Random Walk Down Wall Street*
Douglas McGregor's *The Human Side of Enterprise*
Michael Porter's *Competitive Strategy: Creating and Sustaining Superior Performance*
John Kotter's *Leading Change*
C. K. Prahalad & Gary Hamel's *The Core Competence of the Corporation*

CRIMINOLOGY

Michelle Alexander's *The New Jim Crow: Mass Incarceration in the Age of Colorblindness*
Michael R. Gottfredson & Travis Hirschi's *A General Theory of Crime*
Richard Herrnstein & Charles A. Murray's *The Bell Curve: Intelligence and Class Structure in American Life*
Elizabeth Loftus's *Eyewitness Testimony*
Jay Macleod's *Ain't No Makin' It: Aspirations and Attainment in a Low-Income Neighborhood*
Philip Zimbardo's *The Lucifer Effect*

ECONOMICS

Janet Abu-Lughod's *Before European Hegemony*
Ha-Joon Chang's *Kicking Away the Ladder*
David Brion Davis's *The Problem of Slavery in the Age of Revolution*
Milton Friedman's *The Role of Monetary Policy*
Milton Friedman's *Capitalism and Freedom*
David Graeber's *Debt: the First 5000 Years*
Friedrich Hayek's *The Road to Serfdom*
Karen Ho's *Liquidated: An Ethnography of Wall Street*

The Macat Library By Discipline

John Maynard Keynes's *The General Theory of Employment, Interest and Money*
Charles P. Kindleberger's *Manias, Panics and Crashes*
Robert Lucas's *Why Doesn't Capital Flow from Rich to Poor Countries?*
Burton G. Malkiel's *A Random Walk Down Wall Street*
Thomas Robert Malthus's *An Essay on the Principle of Population*
Karl Marx's *Capital*
Thomas Piketty's *Capital in the Twenty-First Century*
Amartya Sen's *Development as Freedom*
Adam Smith's *The Wealth of Nations*
Nassim Nicholas Taleb's *The Black Swan: The Impact of the Highly Improbable*
Amos Tversky's & Daniel Kahneman's *Judgment under Uncertainty: Heuristics and Biases*
Mahbub Ul Haq's *Reflections on Human Development*
Max Weber's *The Protestant Ethic and the Spirit of Capitalism*

FEMINISM AND GENDER STUDIES

Judith Butler's *Gender Trouble*
Simone De Beauvoir's *The Second Sex*
Michel Foucault's *History of Sexuality*
Betty Friedan's *The Feminine Mystique*
Saba Mahmood's *The Politics of Piety: The Islamic Revival and the Feminist Subject*
Joan Wallach Scott's *Gender and the Politics of History*
Mary Wollstonecraft's *A Vindication of the Rights of Woman*
Virginia Woolf's *A Room of One's Own*

GEOGRAPHY

The Brundtland Report's *Our Common Future*
Rachel Carson's *Silent Spring*
Charles Darwin's *On the Origin of Species*
James Ferguson's *The Anti-Politics Machine*
Jane Jacobs's *The Death and Life of Great American Cities*
James Lovelock's *Gaia: A New Look at Life on Earth*
Amartya Sen's *Development as Freedom*
Mathis Wackernagel & William Rees's *Our Ecological Footprint*

HISTORY

Janet Abu-Lughod's *Before European Hegemony*
Benedict Anderson's *Imagined Communities*
Bernard Bailyn's *The Ideological Origins of the American Revolution*
Hanna Batatu's *The Old Social Classes And The Revolutionary Movements Of Iraq*
Christopher Browning's *Ordinary Men: Reserve Police Batallion 101 and the Final Solution in Poland*
Edmund Burke's *Reflections on the Revolution in France*
William Cronon's *Nature's Metropolis: Chicago And The Great West*
Alfred W. Crosby's *The Columbian Exchange*
Hamid Dabashi's *Iran: A People Interrupted*
David Brion Davis's *The Problem of Slavery in the Age of Revolution*
Nathalie Zemon Davis's *The Return of Martin Guerre*
Jared Diamond's *Guns, Germs & Steel: the Fate of Human Societies*
Frank Dikotter's *Mao's Great Famine*
John W Dower's *War Without Mercy: Race And Power In The Pacific War*
W. E. B. Du Bois's *The Souls of Black Folk*
Richard J. Evans's *In Defence of History*
Lucien Febvre's *The Problem of Unbelief in the 16th Century*
Sheila Fitzpatrick's *Everyday Stalinism*

Eric Foner's *Reconstruction: America's Unfinished Revolution, 1863-1877*
Michel Foucault's *Discipline and Punish*
Michel Foucault's *History of Sexuality*
Francis Fukuyama's *The End of History and the Last Man*
John Lewis Gaddis's *We Now Know: Rethinking Cold War History*
Ernest Gellner's *Nations and Nationalism*
Eugene Genovese's *Roll, Jordan, Roll: The World the Slaves Made*
Carlo Ginzburg's *The Night Battles*
Daniel Goldhagen's *Hitler's Willing Executioners*
Jack Goldstone's *Revolution and Rebellion in the Early Modern World*
Antonio Gramsci's *The Prison Notebooks*
Alexander Hamilton, John Jay & James Madison's *The Federalist Papers*
Christopher Hill's *The World Turned Upside Down*
Carole Hillenbrand's *The Crusades: Islamic Perspectives*
Thomas Hobbes's *Leviathan*
Eric Hobsbawm's *The Age Of Revolution*
John A. Hobson's *Imperialism: A Study*
Albert Hourani's *History of the Arab Peoples*
Samuel P. Huntington's *The Clash of Civilizations and the Remaking of World Order*
C. L. R. James's *The Black Jacobins*
Tony Judt's *Postwar: A History of Europe Since 1945*
Ernst Kantorowicz's *The King's Two Bodies: A Study in Medieval Political Theology*
Paul Kennedy's *The Rise and Fall of the Great Powers*
Ian Kershaw's *The "Hitler Myth": Image and Reality in the Third Reich*
John Maynard Keynes's *The General Theory of Employment, Interest and Money*
Charles P. Kindleberger's *Manias, Panics and Crashes*
Martin Luther King Jr's *Why We Can't Wait*
Henry Kissinger's *World Order: Reflections on the Character of Nations and the Course of History*
Thomas Kuhn's *The Structure of Scientific Revolutions*
Georges Lefebvre's *The Coming of the French Revolution*
John Locke's *Two Treatises of Government*
Niccolò Machiavelli's *The Prince*
Thomas Robert Malthus's *An Essay on the Principle of Population*
Mahmood Mamdani's *Citizen and Subject: Contemporary Africa And The Legacy Of Late Colonialism*
Karl Marx's *Capital*
Stanley Milgram's *Obedience to Authority*
John Stuart Mill's *On Liberty*
Thomas Paine's *Common Sense*
Thomas Paine's *Rights of Man*
Geoffrey Parker's *Global Crisis: War, Climate Change and Catastrophe in the Seventeenth Century*
Jonathan Riley-Smith's *The First Crusade and the Idea of Crusading*
Jean-Jacques Rousseau's *The Social Contract*
Joan Wallach Scott's *Gender and the Politics of History*
Theda Skocpol's *States and Social Revolutions*
Adam Smith's *The Wealth of Nations*
Timothy Snyder's *Bloodlands: Europe Between Hitler and Stalin*
Sun Tzu's *The Art of War*
Keith Thomas's *Religion and the Decline of Magic*
Thucydides's *The History of the Peloponnesian War*
Frederick Jackson Turner's *The Significance of the Frontier in American History*
Odd Arne Westad's *The Global Cold War: Third World Interventions And The Making Of Our Times*

LITERATURE

Chinua Achebe's *An Image of Africa: Racism in Conrad's Heart of Darkness*
Roland Barthes's *Mythologies*
Homi K. Bhabha's *The Location of Culture*
Judith Butler's *Gender Trouble*
Simone De Beauvoir's *The Second Sex*
Ferdinand De Saussure's *Course in General Linguistics*
T. S. Eliot's *The Sacred Wood: Essays on Poetry and Criticism*
Zora Neale Huston's *Characteristics of Negro Expression*
Toni Morrison's *Playing in the Dark: Whiteness in the American Literary Imagination*
Edward Said's *Orientulism*
Gayatri Chakravorty Spivak's *Can the Subaltern Speak?*
Mary Wollstonecraft's *A Vindication of the Rights of Women*
Virginia Woolf's *A Room of One's Own*

PHILOSOPHY

Elizabeth Anscombe's *Modern Moral Philosophy*
Hannah Arendt's *The Human Condition*
Aristotle's *Metaphysics*
Aristotle's *Nicomachean Ethics*
Edmund Gettier's *Is Justified True Belief Knowledge?*
Georg Wilhelm Friedrich Hegel's *Phenomenology of Spirit*
David Hume's *Dialogues Concerning Natural Religion*
David Hume's *The Enquiry for Human Understanding*
Immanuel Kant's *Religion within the Boundaries of Mere Reason*
Immanuel Kant's *Critique of Pure Reason*
Søren Kierkegaard's *The Sickness Unto Death*
Søren Kierkegaard's *Fear and Trembling*
C. S. Lewis's *The Abolition of Man*
Alasdair MacIntyre's *After Virtue*
Marcus Aurelius's *Meditations*
Friedrich Nietzsche's *On the Genealogy of Morality*
Friedrich Nietzsche's *Beyond Good and Evil*
Plato's *Republic*
Plato's *Symposium*
Jean-Jacques Rousseau's *The Social Contract*
Gilbert Ryle's *The Concept of Mind*
Baruch Spinoza's *Ethics*
Sun Tzu's *The Art of War*
Ludwig Wittgenstein's *Philosophical Investigations*

POLITICS

Benedict Anderson's *Imagined Communities*
Aristotle's *Politics*
Bernard Bailyn's *The Ideological Origins of the American Revolution*
Edmund Burke's *Reflections on the Revolution in France*
John C. Calhoun's *A Disquisition on Government*
Ha-Joon Chang's *Kicking Away the Ladder*
Hamid Dabashi's *Iran: A People Interrupted*
Hamid Dabashi's *Theology of Discontent: The Ideological Foundation of the Islamic Revolution in Iran*
Robert Dahl's *Democracy and its Critics*
Robert Dahl's *Who Governs?*
David Brion Davis's *The Problem of Slavery in the Age of Revolution*

Alexis De Tocqueville's *Democracy in America*
James Ferguson's *The Anti-Politics Machine*
Frank Dikotter's *Mao's Great Famine*
Sheila Fitzpatrick's *Everyday Stalinism*
Eric Foner's *Reconstruction: America's Unfinished Revolution, 1863-1877*
Milton Friedman's *Capitalism and Freedom*
Francis Fukuyama's *The End of History and the Last Man*
John Lewis Gaddis's *We Now Know: Rethinking Cold War History*
Ernest Gellner's *Nations and Nationalism*
David Graeber's *Debt: the First 5000 Years*
Antonio Gramsci's *The Prison Notebooks*
Alexander Hamilton, John Jay & James Madison's *The Federalist Papers*
Friedrich Hayek's *The Road to Serfdom*
Christopher Hill's *The World Turned Upside Down*
Thomas Hobbes's *Leviathan*
John A. Hobson's *Imperialism: A Study*
Samuel P. Huntington's *The Clash of Civilizations and the Remaking of World Order*
Tony Judt's *Postwar: A History of Europe Since 1945*
David C. Kang's *China Rising: Peace, Power and Order in East Asia*
Paul Kennedy's *The Rise and Fall of Great Powers*
Robert Keohane's *After Hegemony*
Martin Luther King Jr.'s *Why We Can't Wait*
Henry Kissinger's *World Order: Reflections on the Character of Nations and the Course of History*
John Locke's *Two Treatises of Government*
Niccolò Machiavelli's *The Prince*
Thomas Robert Malthus's *An Essay on the Principle of Population*
Mahmood Mamdani's *Citizen and Subject: Contemporary Africa And The Legacy Of Late Colonialism*
Karl Marx's *Capital*
John Stuart Mill's *On Liberty*
John Stuart Mill's *Utilitarianism*
Hans Morgenthau's *Politics Among Nations*
Thomas Paine's *Common Sense*
Thomas Paine's *Rights of Man*
Thomas Piketty's *Capital in the Twenty-First Century*
Robert D. Putman's *Bowling Alone*
John Rawls's *Theory of Justice*
Jean-Jacques Rousseau's *The Social Contract*
Theda Skocpol's *States and Social Revolutions*
Adam Smith's *The Wealth of Nations*
Sun Tzu's *The Art of War*
Henry David Thoreau's *Civil Disobedience*
Thucydides's *The History of the Peloponnesian War*
Kenneth Waltz's *Theory of International Politics*
Max Weber's *Politics as a Vocation*
Odd Arne Westad's *The Global Cold War: Third World Interventions And The Making Of Our Times*

POSTCOLONIAL STUDIES

Roland Barthes's *Mythologies*
Frantz Fanon's *Black Skin, White Masks*
Homi K. Bhabha's *The Location of Culture*
Gustavo Gutiérrez's *A Theology of Liberation*
Edward Said's *Orientalism*
Gayatri Chakravorty Spivak's *Can the Subaltern Speak?*

PSYCHOLOGY

Gordon Allport's *The Nature of Prejudice*
Alan Baddeley & Graham Hitch's *Aggression: A Social Learning Analysis*
Albert Bandura's *Aggression: A Social Learning Analysis*
Leon Festinger's *A Theory of Cognitive Dissonance*
Sigmund Freud's *The Interpretation of Dreams*
Betty Friedan's *The Feminine Mystique*
Michael R. Gottfredson & Travis Hirschi's *A General Theory of Crime*
Eric Hoffer's *The True Believer: Thoughts on the Nature of Mass Movements*
William James's *Principles of Psychology*
Elizabeth Loftus's *Eyewitness Testimony*
A. H. Maslow's *A Theory of Human Motivation*
Stanley Milgram's *Obedience to Authority*
Steven Pinker's *The Better Angels of Our Nature*
Oliver Sacks's *The Man Who Mistook His Wife For a Hat*
Richard Thaler & Cass Sunstein's *Nudge: Improving Decisions About Health, Wealth and Happiness*
Amos Tversky's *Judgment under Uncertainty: Heuristics and Biases*
Philip Zimbardo's *The Lucifer Effect*

SCIENCE

Rachel Carson's *Silent Spring*
William Cronon's *Nature's Metropolis: Chicago And The Great West*
Alfred W. Crosby's *The Columbian Exchange*
Charles Darwin's *On the Origin of Species*
Richard Dawkin's *The Selfish Gene*
Thomas Kuhn's *The Structure of Scientific Revolutions*
Geoffrey Parker's *Global Crisis: War, Climate Change and Catastrophe in the Seventeenth Century*
Mathis Wackernagel & William Rees's *Our Ecological Footprint*

SOCIOLOGY

Michelle Alexander's *The New Jim Crow: Mass Incarceration in the Age of Colorblindness*
Gordon Allport's *The Nature of Prejudice*
Albert Bandura's *Aggression: A Social Learning Analysis*
Hanna Batatu's *The Old Social Classes And The Revolutionary Movements Of Iraq*
Ha-Joon Chang's *Kicking Away the Ladder*
W. E. B. Du Bois's *The Souls of Black Folk*
Émile Durkheim's *On Suicide*
Frantz Fanon's *Black Skin, White Masks*
Frantz Fanon's *The Wretched of the Earth*
Eric Foner's *Reconstruction: America's Unfinished Revolution, 1863-1877*
Eugene Genovese's *Roll, Jordan, Roll: The World the Slaves Made*
Jack Goldstone's *Revolution and Rebellion in the Early Modern World*
Antonio Gramsci's *The Prison Notebooks*
Richard Herrnstein & Charles A Murray's *The Bell Curve: Intelligence and Class Structure in American Life*
Eric Hoffer's *The True Believer: Thoughts on the Nature of Mass Movements*
Jane Jacobs's *The Death and Life of Great American Cities*
Robert Lucas's *Why Doesn't Capital Flow from Rich to Poor Countries?*
Jay Macleod's *Ain't No Makin' It: Aspirations and Attainment in a Low Income Neighborhood*
Elaine May's *Homeward Bound: American Families in the Cold War Era*
Douglas McGregor's *The Human Side of Enterprise*
C. Wright Mills's *The Sociological Imagination*

Thomas Piketty's *Capital in the Twenty-First Century*
Robert D. Putman's *Bowling Alone*
David Riesman's *The Lonely Crowd: A Study of the Changing American Character*
Edward Said's *Orientalism*
Joan Wallach Scott's *Gender and the Politics of History*
Theda Skocpol's *States and Social Revolutions*
Max Weber's *The Protestant Ethic and the Spirit of Capitalism*

THEOLOGY

Augustine's *Confessions*
Benedict's *Rule of St Benedict*
Gustavo Gutiérrez's *A Theology of Liberation*
Carole Hillenbrand's *The Crusades: Islamic Perspectives*
David Hume's *Dialogues Concerning Natural Religion*
Immanuel Kant's *Religion within the Boundaries of Mere Reason*
Ernst Kantorowicz's *The King's Two Bodies: A Study in Medieval Political Theology*
Søren Kierkegaard's *The Sickness Unto Death*
C. S. Lewis's *The Abolition of Man*
Saba Mahmood's *The Politics of Piety: The Islamic Revival and the Feminist Subject*
Baruch Spinoza's *Ethics*
Keith Thomas's *Religion and the Decline of Magic*

COMING SOON

Chris Argyris's *The Individual and the Organisation*
Seyla Benhabib's *The Rights of Others*
Walter Benjamin's *The Work Of Art in the Age of Mechanical Reproduction*
John Berger's *Ways of Seeing*
Pierre Bourdieu's *Outline of a Theory of Practice*
Mary Douglas's *Purity and Danger*
Roland Dworkin's *Taking Rights Seriously*
James G. March's *Exploration and Exploitation in Organisational Learning*
Ikujiro Nonaka's *A Dynamic Theory of Organizational Knowledge Creation*
Griselda Pollock's *Vision and Difference*
Amartya Sen's *Inequality Re-Examined*
Susan Sontag's *On Photography*
Yasser Tabbaa's *The Transformation of Islamic Art*
Ludwig von Mises's *Theory of Money and Credit*

Macat Disciplines

Access the greatest ideas and thinkers across entire disciplines, including

Postcolonial Studies

Roland Barthes's *Mythologies*
Frantz Fanon's *Black Skin, White Masks*
Homi K. Bhabha's *The Location of Culture*
Gustavo Gutiérrez's *A Theology of Liberation*
Edward Said's *Orientalism*
Gayatri Chakravorty Spivak's *Can the Subaltern Speak?*

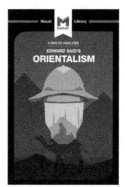

Macat Disciplines

Access the greatest ideas and thinkers across entire disciplines, including

AFRICANA STUDIES

Chinua Achebe's *An Image of Africa: Racism in Conrad's Heart of Darkness*

W. E. B. Du Bois's *The Souls of Black Folk*

Zora Neale Hurston's *Characteristics of Negro Expression*

Martin Luther King Jr.'s *Why We Can't Wait*

Toni Morrison's *Playing in the Dark: Whiteness in the American Literary Imagination*

Macat analyses are available from all good bookshops and libraries.

Access hundreds of analyses through one, multimedia tool.
Join free for one month **library.macat.com**

Macat Disciplines

Access the greatest ideas and thinkers across entire disciplines, including

FEMINISM, GENDER AND QUEER STUDIES

Simone De Beauvoir's
The Second Sex

Michel Foucault's
History of Sexuality

Betty Friedan's
The Feminine Mystique

Saba Mahmood's
*The Politics of Piety:
The Islamic Revival and
the Feminist Subject*

Joan Wallach Scott's
*Gender and the
Politics of History*

Mary Wollstonecraft's
*A Vindication of the
Rights of Woman*

Virginia Woolf's
A Room of One's Own

Judith Butler's
Gender Trouble

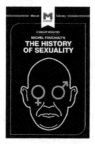

Macat Disciplines

Access the greatest ideas and thinkers across entire disciplines, including

CRIMINOLOGY

Michelle Alexander's
The New Jim Crow: Mass Incarceration in the Age of Colorblindness

Michael R. Gottfredson & Travis Hirschi's
A General Theory of Crime

Elizabeth Loftus's
Eyewitness Testimony

Richard Herrnstein & Charles A. Murray's
The Bell Curve: Intelligence and Class Structure in American Life

Jay Macleod's
Ain't No Makin' It: Aspirations and Attainment in a Low-Income Neighborhood

Philip Zimbardo's
The Lucifer Effect

Macat Disciplines

Access the greatest ideas and thinkers across entire disciplines, including

INEQUALITY

Ha-Joon Chang's, *Kicking Away the Ladder*
David Graeber's, *Debt: The First 5000 Years*
Robert E. Lucas's, *Why Doesn't Capital Flow from Rich To Poor Countries?*
Thomas Piketty's, *Capital in the Twenty-First Century*
Amartya Sen's, *Inequality Re-Examined*
Mahbub Ul Haq's, *Reflections on Human Development*

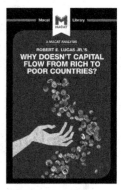

Macat analyses are available from all good bookshops and libraries.

Access hundreds of analyses through one, multimedia tool.
Join free for one month **library.macat.com**

Macat Disciplines

Access the greatest ideas and thinkers across entire disciplines, including

GLOBALIZATION

Arjun Appadurai's, *Modernity at Large: Cultural Dimensions of Globalisation*

James Ferguson's, *The Anti-Politics Machine*

Geert Hofstede's, *Culture's Consequences*

Amartya Sen's, *Development as Freedom*

Macat analyses are available from all good bookshops and libraries.

Access hundreds of analyses through one, multimedia tool.
Join free for one month **library.macat.com**

Macat Disciplines

Access the greatest ideas and thinkers across entire disciplines, including

MAN AND THE ENVIRONMENT

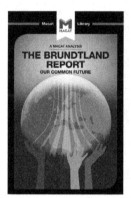

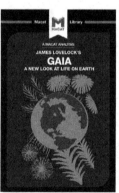
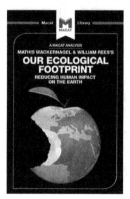

The Brundtland Report's, *Our Common Future*
Rachel Carson's, *Silent Spring*
James Lovelock's, *Gaia: A New Look at Life on Earth*
Mathis Wackernagel & William Rees's, *Our Ecological Footprint*

Macat analyses are available from all good bookshops and libraries.

Access hundreds of analyses through one, multimedia tool.
Join free for one month **library.macat.com**

Macat Disciplines
Access the greatest ideas and thinkers across entire disciplines, including

THE FUTURE OF DEMOCRACY

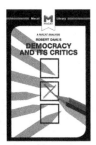   

Robert A. Dahl's, *Democracy and Its Critics*
Robert A. Dahl's, *Who Governs?*
Alexis De Toqueville's, *Democracy in America*
Niccolò Machiavelli's, *The Prince*
John Stuart Mill's, *On Liberty*
Robert D. Putnam's, *Bowling Alone*
Jean-Jacques Rousseau's, *The Social Contract*
Henry David Thoreau's, *Civil Disobedience*

Macat Disciplines

Access the greatest ideas and thinkers across entire disciplines, including

TOTALITARIANISM

Sheila Fitzpatrick's, *Everyday Stalinism*
Ian Kershaw's, *The "Hitler Myth"*
Timothy Snyder's, *Bloodlands*

Macat Pairs

Analyse historical and modern issues from opposite sides of an argument. Pairs include:

RACE AND IDENTITY

Zora Neale Hurston's
Characteristics of Negro Expression

Using material collected on anthropological expeditions to the South, Zora Neale Hurston explains how expression in African American culture in the early twentieth century departs from the art of white America. At the time, African American art was often criticized for copying white culture. For Hurston, this criticism misunderstood how art works. European tradition views art as something fixed. But Hurston describes a creative process that is alive, ever-changing, and largely improvisational. She maintains that African American art works through a process called 'mimicry'—where an imitated object or verbal pattern, for example, is reshaped and altered until it becomes something new, novel—and worthy of attention.

Frantz Fanon's
Black Skin, White Masks

Black Skin, White Masks offers a radical analysis of the psychological effects of colonization on the colonized.

Fanon witnessed the effects of colonization first hand both in his birthplace, Martinique, and again later in life when he worked as a psychiatrist in another French colony, Algeria. His text is uncompromising in form and argument. He dissects the dehumanizing effects of colonialism, arguing that it destroys the native sense of identity, forcing people to adapt to an alien set of values—including a core belief that they are inferior. This results in deep psychological trauma.

Fanon's work played a pivotal role in the civil rights movements of the 1960s.

Macat Pairs

Analyse historical and modern issues from opposite sides of an argument. Pairs include:

INTERNATIONAL RELATIONS IN THE 21ST CENTURY

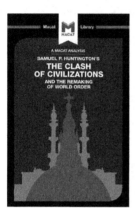

Samuel P. Huntington's
The Clash of Civilisations

In his highly influential 1996 book, Huntington offers a vision of a post-Cold War world in which conflict takes place not between competing ideologies but between cultures. The worst clash, he argues, will be between the Islamic world and the West: the West's arrogance and belief that its culture is a "gift" to the world will come into conflict with Islam's obstinacy and concern that its culture is under attack from a morally decadent "other."

Clash inspired much debate between different political schools of thought. But its greatest impact came in helping define American foreign policy in the wake of the 2001 terrorist attacks in New York and Washington.

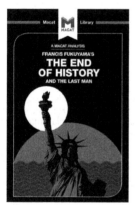

Francis Fukuyama's
The End of History and the Last Man

Published in 1992, *The End of History and the Last Man* argues that capitalist democracy is the final destination for all societies. Fukuyama believed democracy triumphed during the Cold War because it lacks the "fundamental contradictions" inherent in communism and satisfies our yearning for freedom and equality. Democracy therefore marks the endpoint in the evolution of ideology, and so the "end of history." There will still be "events," but no fundamental change in ideology.

Macat Pairs

Analyse historical and modern issues from opposite sides of an argument. Pairs include:

HOW TO RUN AN ECONOMY

John Maynard Keynes's
The General Theory OF Employment, Interest and Money

Classical economics suggests that market economies are self-correcting in times of recession or depression, and tend toward full employment and output. But English economist John Maynard Keynes disagrees.

In his ground-breaking 1936 study *The General Theory*, Keynes argues that traditional economics has misunderstood the causes of unemployment. Employment is not determined by the price of labor; it is directly linked to demand. Keynes believes market economies are by nature unstable, and so require government intervention. Spurred on by the social catastrophe of the Great Depression of the 1930s, he sets out to revolutionize the way the world thinks

Milton Friedman's
The Role of Monetary Policy

Friedman's 1968 paper changed the course of economic theory. In just 17 pages, he demolished existing theory and outlined an effective alternate monetary policy designed to secure 'high employment, stable prices and rapid growth.'

Friedman demonstrated that monetary policy plays a vital role in broader economic stability and argued that economists got their monetary policy wrong in the 1950s and 1960s by misunderstanding the relationship between inflation and unemployment. Previous generations of economists had believed that governments could permanently decrease unemployment by permitting inflation—and vice versa. Friedman's most original contribution was to show that this supposed trade-off is an illusion that only works in the short term.

Macat Pairs

*Analyse historical and modern issues
from opposite sides of an argument.
Pairs include:*

ARE WE FUNDAMENTALLY GOOD - OR BAD?

Steven Pinker's
The Better Angels of Our Nature

Stephen Pinker's gloriously optimistic 2011 book argues that, despite humanity's biological tendency toward violence, we are, in fact, less violent today than ever before. To prove his case, Pinker lays out pages of detailed statistical evidence. For him, much of the credit for the decline goes to the eighteenth-century Enlightenment movement, whose ideas of liberty, tolerance, and respect for the value of human life filtered down through society and affected how people thought. That psychological change led to behavioral change—and overall we became more peaceful. Critics countered that humanity could never overcome the biological urge toward violence; others argued that Pinker's statistics were flawed.

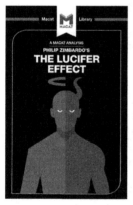

Philip Zimbardo's
The Lucifer Effect

Some psychologists believe those who commit cruelty are innately evil. Zimbardo disagrees. In *The Lucifer Effect*, he argues that sometimes good people do evil things simply because of the situations they find themselves in, citing many historical examples to illustrate his point. Zimbardo details his 1971 Stanford prison experiment, where ordinary volunteers playing guards in a mock prison rapidly became abusive. But he also describes the tortures committed by US army personnel in Iraq's Abu Ghraib prison in 2003—and how he himself testified in defence of one of those guards. committed by US army personnel in Iraq's Abu Ghraib prison in 2003—and how he himself testified in defence of one of those guards.

Macat analyses are available from all good bookshops and libraries.

Access hundreds of analyses through one, multimedia tool.
Join free for one month **library.macat.com**

Macat Pairs

Analyse historical and modern issues from opposite sides of an argument. Pairs include:

HOW WE RELATE TO EACH OTHER AND SOCIETY

Jean-Jacques Rousseau's
The Social Contract

Rousseau's famous work sets out the radical concept of the 'social contract': a give-and-take relationship between individual freedom and social order.

If people are free to do as they like, governed only by their own sense of justice, they are also vulnerable to chaos and violence. To avoid this, Rousseau proposes, they should agree to give up some freedom to benefit from the protection of social and political organization. But this deal is only just if societies are led by the collective needs and desires of the people, and able to control the private interests of individuals. For Rousseau, the only legitimate form of government is rule by the people.

Robert D. Putnam's
Bowling Alone

In *Bowling Alone*, Robert Putnam argues that Americans have become disconnected from one another and from the institutions of their common life, and investigates the consequences of this change.

Looking at a range of indicators, from membership in formal organizations to the number of invitations being extended to informal dinner parties, Putnam demonstrates that Americans are interacting less and creating less "social capital" – with potentially disastrous implications for their society.

It would be difficult to overstate the impact of *Bowling Alone*, one of the most frequently cited social science publications of the last half-century.

Printed in the United States
by Baker & Taylor Publisher Services